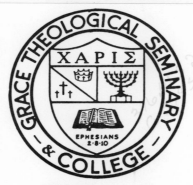

THE
Small Business Legal Problem Solver

THE
Small Business
Legal Problem Solver

Arnold S. Goldstein

Inc./CBI Publications
286 Congress Street
Boston, Massachusetts 02210

Library of Congress Cataloging in Publication Data

Goldstein, Arnold S.
  The small business legal problem solver.

  Includes index.
    1. Small business—Law and legislation—United
  States. I. Title.
KF1659.G64 1983   346.73'0652   82-20692
ISBN 0-8436-0890-0   347.306652
ISBN 0-8436-0891-9 (pbk.)

Printed in the United States of America

Printing *(last digit):* 9 8 7 6 5 4 3 2 1

To my wife, Marlene, for her tireless effort and encouragement in assisting me in the preparation of this book.

CONTENTS

PREFACE

Know the law, and you know the rules by which the game of business is played. To succeed and to avoid costly mistakes, you must have a solid understanding of these rules. That's what this book is all about. It's a reference guide that can give you immediate, comprehensive, and easy-to-follow answers to your most common business law problems.

It's a valuable handbook for every business owner. Whether you own and operate a corner store or a large manufacturing conglomerate, it can help you. Executives and management staff can benefit from material relating to every phase of business operation. Its advice is even useful for attorneys, accountants, and consultants looking for better ways to handle and explain the most complex legal matters for their clients.

To accomplish these objectives, I have taken a specific, and perhaps a unique, approach to making this book more valuable to you. First, I use a question-and-answer format. Virtually all other law books state the law in narrative form. This makes it difficult for nonlawyers to find the right legal principles to apply to their questions. The questions in this book will parallel your own, and with the questions, I give you the answers. The format allows me to put it all in context for you.

I have focused in on the most common and important legal questions. I don't promise that you'll find the answer to every conceivable legal question, and I doubt whether any one book can provide that. But by selecting the most common questions, I can give you comprehensive answers, and that's far more useful than a superficial treatment encompassing your less likely problems.

Most legal jargon has been eliminated, or at least carefully defined for you. I give you the answers just as I would if you were sitting across from my desk. That means I have to tell you my answers so that you can understand them. To assist you further, I include a comprehensive legal glossary at the end of the book.

This book doesn't merely state the law; it goes far beyond that. It tells you what to do and what not to do. I give you step-by-step instructions showing you precisely how to solve your problems. You will find the extensive checklists useful, and the examples showing what other business people have done to solve the same problems can only serve to clarify your options.

Comprehensiveness is another hallmark of this book. Glance at the Contents, and you will find that the book covers everything from how to start-up to how to sell or liquidate your business, and of course it covers all the common day-to-day operational problems you will have while you are in business.

Finally, this book has one more unique characteristic—practicality. The law may be the rules by which business is conducted, but it's nevertheless only one dimension to effective management. I interject the options available to you so that you know not only your legal rights but also the option that may be best for effective management. Therefore, you will find a blend of "no-nonsense management" coupled with the law.

A strong word of caution: On complex or important legal questions, use the book as a supplement but always follow the advice of your counsel. This book can help you solve your day-to-day problems and even help you decide when legal advice is necessary. Only your counsel, however, can consider all the facts, apply the specific laws of your state, and give you the protection you need on matters of importance.

Read this book from cover to cover. You will see ready answers to many of the questions you have or will have. You will find more effective ways to handle your problems. You may even discover costly errors that you are making, with guidance on correcting them.

When you have a specific problem, turn to the appropriate section. Look up the question that parallels your own. By keeping this book on your desk, you will have at your fingertips immediate and easy-to-understand answers to your most common legal problems.

NOTE

This publication is designed to provide accurate and authoritative information in regard to the subject matter covered. It is sold with the understanding that the publisher is not engaged in rendering legal, accounting, or other professional service. If legal advice or other expert assistance is required, the services of a competent professional person should be sought.

From a declaration of principles jointly adopted by a committee of the American Bar Association and a committee of Publishers and Associations.

CHAPTER

1

You and Your Organization

1.1 WHAT A CORPORATION WILL DO FOR YOU

Q. *I find conflicting opinions as to whether to incorporate a business or conduct it as a nonincorporated proprietorship. What are your views on the subject?*

A. From my experiences, a corporation is essential. The advantages are all on the side of the corporation. Here's support for my statement.

1. *Limited liability*: The corporation is the only form of business organization that can limit your personal loss or risk to whatever you invest. Under a proprietorship you are personally liable for all of your business's indebtedness, and its creditors can look to your personal assets for full satisfaction. This is the one reason why most small business owners do incorporate.

2. *Fringe benefits*: A corporation can provide valuable, tax-deductible "fringes," including sick pay; medical, dental, and hospitalization plans; life insurance; and perhaps even educational costs, and travel and moving expenses. Your accountant can review these possibilities with you.

3. *Workers' compensation coverage*: Operate under a corporation, and you are eligible as an employee for workers' compensation insurance coverage. The cost will be negligible, but the benefits are extremely valuable. As a proprietor, you are the employer and are not covered.

4. *Survivorship*: As a distinct legal entity, the corporation survives you. You can bequest your shares with no interruption of the business. Under a proprietorship, the business legally terminates upon your death and will have to be sold or liquidated.

5. *Taxes*: Most people believe the corporation offers tax disadvantages. In actuality, however, it offers only potential advantages. You can elect to be taxed as a "sole proprietorship" under a "Sub-Chapter S" corporation (see question 11.3). This will give you precisely the same tax treatment you would enjoy if you were not incorporated. The corporation may, however, effect its own tax benefits. Therefore, the corporation can never represent a tax "disadvantage."

6. *Division of ownership*: Should you want to bring in other investors, it will be appreciably easier to do it with a corporation. The corporate structure lends itself to multiple ownership or creative financing.

The only disadvantage to incorporating is the few hundred dollars you may have to pay each year for filing fees and corporate tax preparation. But that's a small price to pay for what a corporation can do for you.

1.2 THE FIVE MAJOR DISADVANTAGES OF PARTNERSHIP ORGANIZATIONS

Q. *Many lawyers do not recommend the partnership form of organization, suggesting instead that the partners "incorporate" as costockholders. Isn't a partnership form of organization an easier method for going into business?*

A. Although I haven't conducted a survey, I'm confident that virtually all lawyers recommend a corporation over a partnership. The reasons for this are compelling.

1. The partnership creates unlimited personal liability for each partner. If the business goes bankrupt, the creditors can recover against all or any one partner.

2. Any partner can bind the other partners personally to business debts, contracts, or legal actions. You may become the victim of your partners' actions.

3. A partnership is automatically terminated by the death or withdrawal of any one partner. That not only forces the surviving partners to buy out the deceased partner's interest, but it can also cause problems in reorganizing the business and getting it started again.

4. Profits of the business are taxed pro rata to the partners, whether they have taken the profits from the business or not.

5. You cannot change any of these disadvantages by a partnership agreement, as these conditions exist by law.

Many business people choose a partnership to avoid paying several hundred dollars to incorporate. They are fooling themselves, for their failure to incorporate can be a costly mistake, and in fact most attorneys charge more to prepare a partnership agreement than a corporation. So you may find it's both easier and less expensive to incorporate.

Don't, however, confuse a general partnership with a limited partnership. Limited partnerships are used extensively for real estate investments and are highly advantageous, as the limited partners cannot be liable for partnership debts and have the tax deductions that real estate as a tax shelter can provide.

1.3 SMALL BUSINESS ACQUISITIONS— STOCK OR ASSETS?

Q. *I have been negotiating for several months to buy a small incorporated restaurant. I know I can accomplish the takeover either through buying all the shares of the seller's corporation or through setting up my own corporation and having the seller transfer all the assets to mine. What are the pros and cons of each method?*

A. In most cases I favor the purchase of assets, although in certain cases it may make more sense to buy the shares. Here are the factors to consider if you purchase assets.

1. You don't have to worry about any "hidden" liability that the seller's corporation may have.

2. You may be able to allocate a significant part of the purchase price to capital assets, which can give you a high beginning basis for depreciation.

3. You won't have to worry about union contracts or contractual agreements to which the selling corporation is bound.

On the other hand, buying a corporation means considering these factors.

1. You may be able to continue with a seller's favorable lease rather than negotiate with the landlord for a new lease.

2. "Takeover financing" may be in place, whereas you may have to pay off the seller's loans with your own financing if you acquire assets.

3. You may have the advantage of a tax loss carryforward.

4. The corporation may have an excellent credit rating that can help you.

Here's the approach to use. Qualify the tax, finance, and new lease cost implications and reduce them to a probable dollar amount. Against this, weigh the risk of "hidden" liabilities. If the purchase of stock shows an economic benefit and you have adequate recourse against the seller for unlisted (hidden) liabilities, then the risk/benefit ratio is in your favor, and you should buy the seller's corporation.

Perhaps the best way to protect yourself from "hidden" liabilities is to have the seller finance a substantial part of the purchase price and provide in the promissory note that you can "deduct" from the next due installments any "hidden" (unlisted) liabilities that may arise and are not discharged by the seller.

Your decision will require careful analysis by both your attorney and your accountant.

1.4 SHOULD YOU INCORPORATE IN DELAWARE?

Q. *We are planning to incorporate our furniture plant in Georgia. I have always heard that we could incorporate in Delaware and enjoy excellent benefits, even if the company is located in another state. What are the advantages of incorporating in Delaware?*

A. Delaware does offer some attractive inducements.

1. Delaware has no corporate income tax on nonresident corporations and no tax on shares or inheritance for nonresident stockholders.

2. You don't have to hold stockholders' and directors' meetings within Delaware.

3. Delaware has no minimal capital requirements.

4. A Delaware corporation can hold securities in its own or any other corporation.

5. Dividends can be paid out of profits as well as surplus, which is the big advantage.

Some of these advantages can justify incorporating in Delaware, but as a practical matter only the larger firms and banking institutions can really benefit.

As a Delaware corporation operating in Georgia, you may still have to pay taxes to Georgia. You should therefore have your accountant investigate whether you would actually save taxes through Delaware incorporation.

1.5 YOUR CHECKLIST WHEN DOING BUSINESS IN ANOTHER STATE

Q. *We sell to retail accounts in several states. We are not certain whether we have to register as a "foreign corporation"* *in those states. At what point are we subject to liability if we don't register?*

A. Whether you will be obligated to register as a foreign corporation will depend on the degree of involvement your business has in that state and on the individual state laws.

No absolute rules exist to determine what constitutes "doing enough business" to subject you to the requirements of filing as a corporation in another state. Any of the following, however, may apply. Ask yourself these questions.

1. Do you maintain a branch office, telephone number, post office box, or bank account in this state?

2. Do you maintain physical assets within the state?

3. Do you conduct a continuing course of business to regular accounts?

4. Are you involved in licensing or franchising within the state?

Most cases provide that solicitation of orders within a state, to be shipped from outside the state, do not require filing as a foreign corporation.

You should check with the department of corporations for each state in which you regularly conduct business to determine whether registration is required and whether your company is liable for any sales, use, or personal property taxes.

If you are required to register but fail to do so, you may suffer serious sanctions. Among such sanctions are the following.

1. You may have to pay penalties on taxes due the state.

2. You may have to pay penalties for failure to qualify as a foreign corporation.

3. You may be unable to use the state courts to enforce any contracts with accounts within the state.

1.6 WHAT YOU—NOT YOUR CORPORATION—SHOULD OWN

Q. *After several years of owning our supermarket, we finally have the opportunity to buy the building. We are undecided about whether to buy the building in our own names or have it owned by the corporation. What are your recommendations?*

A. The answer to that question will depend on two important considerations:

- Risk of loss if the business fails
- Tax consequences

Owners of closely held businesses should avoid having their operating companies own the real estate, as the real estate will be lost if the corporation becomes insolvent. Consider the statistics. Over 80 percent of all small businesses fail. The objective then is to own the real estate personally so that the business creditors will not have recourse to it should your business experience financial trouble.

Of course, publicly held corporations don't have that option, as they have other stockholders to answer to. You, as a sole stockholder, do have that option, and you can even have the corporation advance the down payment. One procedure would be to "borrow" the down payment from the corporation (structure it as a legitimate loan so that it's not taxed as dividend income) and repay the loan from the profits on rents.

Once you own the building, you should structure a fair and reasonable lease between you and the corporation. Be certain to obtain an independent appraisal on the rental value so that the IRS can't contest the legitimacy of the rent.

Through personal ownership of the building, you'll have the advantage of the tax deductions that investment real estate offers. Your accountant can calculate the tax benefits through personal, rather than corporate, ownership as they apply to your specific situation.

With few exceptions real estate should be personally owned. I recommend that business owners also consider personal ownership of these assets.

1. *Valuable patents and trademarks*: You can grant the corporation an exclusive license.

2. *Specific high-cost equipment*: As with real estate, this can be leased to the corporation.

Review the assets your corporation owns or may acquire. Have your accountant and attorney guide you on the advantages of personal rather than corporate ownership.

1.7 WHAT YOU AND YOUR PARTNER MUST AGREE ON

Q. *After working as a car salesperson for a number of years, I have an opportunity to buy into partnership in a car dealership. What provisions should the partnership agreement contain?*

A. If you are planning a "partnership" form of organization, I'd be opposed to it, and I tell you why under question 1.2. The only form of business organization that can give you the necessary protection is a corporation.

But let's assume that you and your partner do incorporate as costockholders. You will have to agree on the basic points of your relationship before you start. You can't rely on corporate bylaws to give you the functional guidelines that create the "meeting of the minds" between partners. That's precisely why so many partnerships do fail (whether incorporated or not): The partners lacked adequate discussion and agreement between them on the key points. Before you go into the deal, agree on these all-important issues.

1. How much will each partner invest? When will it be paid? Will additional capital be available if needed, perhaps for

expansion purposes? Try to choose a partner with equal financial resources.

2. Define what percentage of the business each partner will own. Be wary of a minority interest (see question 3.19).

3. Agree on the time commitments. I have seen many partnerships fail because one partner was willing to work only 30 to 40 hours a week while the other decided that 60 hours a week were necessary.

4. Determine who will do what. Management functions will be divided to some extent so that division of responsibility should be decided beforehand.

5. Decide on a "game plan." How will the business be operated? What basic strategies will be used? Where is the business going, and how will it get there? These questions are fundamental if the business is to succeed.

6. Who will have what authority? For example, who has authority to enter into important contracts or to write checks?

7. What will be the salaries? It's amazing to find how few partners never even discuss this until after they're in business. Make certain the salaries you do agree on can be easily paid by the business.

8. What are the provisions for dissolution? It's best to decide the ways and means before you start. How will you arbitrate disagreements? What about a "buy-out" provision if the partnership is to be terminated? In the event of death, what happens? (See question 1.10 for some valuable ideas.)

You may have some other questions to ask and issues to decide, but the point is to consider your partnership a marriage. That requires you and your partner to know what you expect, both from each other and from the business.

1.8   THE SAFEST WAY TO ORGANIZE MULTIOPERATION BUSINESSES

Q.   *We presently own two fast-food operations and plan on opening two additional units within the next year. Our existing businesses are both owned and operated under one corporation. Do you suggest using the same corporation to open the next two?*

A.   No. Any business operator with multiple businesses should consider using a separate corporation for each.

This has one major advantage. If one business should fail, it will not jeopardize the others, as the creditors of the defunct business will only have recourse to its assets and not to the assets of the other businesses. By having one corporation own all four businesses, you risk them all should any one fail. Furthermore, as you expand, you will likely find that "losing proposition" that you'll want to shed with minimum loss.

You also have nothing to lose in taxes. You should set up a "holding corporation" that will own the shares of your four "subsidiary corporations." Under federal tax laws, you will be able to file one consolidated tax return for all four corporations, so the losses of one or more can be used to offset the profits of the others. You may, however, be required to file separate state tax returns.

To obtain the protection of operating separate corporations, you must operate them as distinct entities. Make certain that you adhere to these guidelines.

1. Keep separate books and records for each corporation.

2. Don't commingle funds. Each corporation should have its own checking account.

3. Pay bills for each corporation from its own funds. You can use a central checking account or a computer system as long as you can segregate the sources of income and allocate the disbursements to each of the four corporations.

4. Carefully document transfers of merchandise between stores and maintain intercompany receivables and payable ledgers.

5. Have suppliers bill each corporation separately.

Sound business practice requires you to follow this same procedure even if you operate all four stores under one corporation. It is, after all, the only way you can measure the profitability of each.

1.9   HOW TO CONTROL VOTING RIGHTS IN A SMALL CORPORATION

Q.   *I want to control voting rights in a wholesale jewelry corporation. I currently own 100 percent of the stock but need an infusion of capital that an "incoming" stockholder will provide. In return for a $50,000 investment, this stockholder wants 50 percent of the ownership. I don't think the new stockholder would object to my controlling the corporation. How can this be accomplished?*

A.   You have two methods to accomplish your goal.

1. Issue to your stockholder 50 percent of the stock but have your new partner give you a nonrevocable proxy to vote some of these shares.

2. Issue two different classes of stock. You may own 50 shares of class A (voting shares), and your partner may own 50 shares of class B (nonvoting shares). That, of course, would give you all the voting rights, but if your partner wanted some voting rights, you might take 51 percent of class A and 40 percent of class B and give up the reciprocal amount of each class. This way you end up with a simple majority of the class A shares but only 50 percent of the total shares.

What you have to decide is the percentage of the voting shares you demand. Fifty-one percent will give you control of electing directors and of day-to-day decision making, but it may not be enough to give you total control. Most states require a 67 percent stockholder vote to make material changes in the structure, such as

- Changing the name, location, or purpose of the corporation
- Mortgaging or selling all or substantially all the assets
- Leasing premises for the corporation
- Liquidation or dissolution.

In addition your own bylaws may require something more than a 51 percent vote to undertake certain actions.

The key is to know precisely what degree of control you want and to make certain that you have it.

1.10 HOW TO PURCHASE EFFECTIVELY THE INTEREST OF A DECEASED PARTNER

Q. *I own 50 percent of the shares in a chain of stereo shops, and my partner of 12 years owns the remaining shares. What is the best way to provide for the transfer of the shares to the other, should one of us die?*

A. The common solution is called the "cross-partnership" (or stockholder) buy-out agreement. Here's how it works.

1. You and your partner agree on the value of the business. Assuming the net worth (assets less liabilities) is $200,000, you would have respective interests valued at $100,000.

2. You and your partner each take out a life insurance policy for $100,000 dollars and name the other partner as beneficiary.

3. Your attorney drafts an agreement stating that upon the death of a stockholder, the estate will agree to sell this stock-

holder's shares to the survivor. In turn, the surviving stockholder would be obligated to take the life insurance proceeds and use them to buy the shares. The surviving partner would then have 100 percent of the shares; the estate of the deceased stockholder would immediately obtain the fair value for the shares; and the best part is that the entire transaction would be funded by the insurance proceeds.

A variation of this approach is called the "entity" plan. With this method, each stockholder names the corporation as the beneficiary, and the corporation is obligated to buy the deceased stockholder's shares and retire the shares as nonvoting treasury stock. Of course, once the transactions are completed, the surviving stockholder still owns 100 percent of the outstanding voting shares.

Although both methods achieve the same objective, the difference is in the tax deductibility of the insurance premiums. Under the entity plan the corporation may be able to pay the premiums and write them off as deductible expense, but you should review this carefully with your accountant.

The main point to remember is that you and your partner will have to revalue the business at least once a year and establish a new buy-out price based on the most recent valuation. You will then have to modify the insurance coverage to coincide with that value. The plan will require the know-how of many experts.

1. *You and your partner*: Together you establish the value of the business—annually.

2. *Your insurance broker*: Your broker designs the appropriate insurance coverage.

3. *Your attorney*: An attorney should draft the "buy/sell" agreement.

4. *Your accountant*: You will need to make certain you obtain the maximum tax benefits.

Virtually all professional advisors recommend insurance-funded buy-out agreements as the best way to handle the

transfer of a business interest to surviving partners. It's the
only method that will

- Avoid subsequent disputes over the value of the deceased
  partner's interest
- Provide immediate cash for the buy-out
- Give the surviving partners full ownership on a fully
  paid basis, without personal investment or expensive
  borrowing.

1.11 HOW TO PREVENT CONFLICTS BETWEEN A DIRECTOR AND THE CORPORATION

Q. *As president of a manufacturing plant, I have just
learned that one of our directors personally purchased the real
estate within which our plant is located. I doubt that our
company would have been interested in buying it, but I believe
the director should have given us the opportunity to consider
it. Do you agree?*

A.   Absolutely. A director (and all officers) have a "fiduciary
duty" to their corporation. They owe it the highest degree of
loyalty and fidelity. Given this theory, the director had the
duty first to present to the corporation all opportunities that
could possibly be of benefit to the company before exploiting
them for personal gain.

You may be able to force the director to resell the property
to the corporation for the purchase price on the basis that the
breach of fiduciary duty caused the corporation a "loss of corporate opportunity." Directors and officers engaged in potential conflicts with the corporation should follow this checklist.

1. First, present all opportunities or areas of potential conflict to the other directors at a board of directors meeting and
fully disclose all the details of the opportunity or conflict.

2. Give the corporation full opportunity to act on the situation.

3. If the director contemplates taking advantage of the opportunity should the corporation decline it, then that fact should be made known at the outset, and the director should refrain from voting on behalf of the corporation.

4. A director (or officer) who controls the board of directors should obtain a waiver from the stockholders.

5. Once the corporation declines, the director can proceed to acquire the property. If, however, the director is able to acquire the property on terms different from those originally stated, the board should be given the opportunity for a new vote.

6. Once the property is acquired by the director, then this director has an obvious conflict with the corporation and must decline attendance or voting on any matters relating to the conflict (in this case the lessor–lessee relationship).

7. Any resale by the director should provide a "right of first refusal" to the corporation.

The corporation should keep detailed minutes of the meetings to record this chronology of events, and the director should also retain a copy.

1.12 PROTECTING YOURSELF FROM IMPROPER DEMANDS TO INSPECT BOOKS

Q. *Our electronics firm has its stock traded "over-the-counter." One of our competitors purchased a few shares of our stock and now wants to inspect our books. Do they have the right to demand inspection?*

A. Stockholders have the right to inspect books, as long as it's for a proper purpose. In this case you can limit the information only to accounting information and certainly are not obligated to disclose "trade secrets" or other confidential information that should be confined to the management.

If demand is made to see any records that could give your "stockholder" a competitive advantage, then you should refuse disclosure unless your competitor obtains a court order. In fact, providing confidential or classified information without a court order could create liability for you, as other stockholders may claim you breached your duties to the corporation by inadequately safeguarding this information. Courts routinely allow stockholders access to these items.

- Lists of stockholders (A stockholder always has the right to communicate with other stockholders, even if it's for purposes of "unseating" the present management.)
- Relevant books, records of account, and corporate minutes
- Tax returns and financial statements
- Contracts with officers and key employees.

Further, a stockholder has the right to make photostatic copies of these documents (at personal expense) or to make extracts from these records. You have the right to reasonable notice before inspection and should confine the inspection to the premises of the company during normal working hours. You also have the right to have a representative of the company present during the inspection.

Some states impose a penalty of up to 10 percent of the value of the shares of the stockholder demanding inspection if you wrongfully refuse. Considering your obligations to preserve confidential information on one hand and to comply with lawful inspection demands on the other, you should refer any questionable demands to corporate counsel for determination.

1.13   CAN YOU FORCE A CORPORATION TO PAY A DIVIDEND

Q.   *Two years ago I invested $100,000 for shares in an "over-the-counter" corporation. The corporation has earned over $250,000 in the past five years and still has not paid a dividend. Can I go to court to compel the directors to pay a dividend?*

A.   You can go to court, but you won't be successful. First, dividends are not payable out of profits but are paid from surplus. The term "surplus" means the book value of the assets minus the liabilities and capital stock. The retained earnings of the corporation would be the surplus.

It may be that in prior years the corporation operated at a loss, and even with the $250,000 in profits in recent years, the corporation may still have a negative retained earnings, or surplus, and therefore it would be illegal for the directors to declare a dividend. Some states, such as Delaware, do allow directors to pay dividends from profits rather than surplus, but these states are in the minority. In fact, directors who do declare a dividend illegally can be personally liable to creditors. So your first step is to make certain that the corporation has retained earnings justifying the payment of dividends.

Even if the corporation has retained earnings, the directors enjoy full discretion on the question of dividends. In very few cases have the courts overturned the directors' judgment, and in those few cases the accumulated surplus was so substantial that the directors could not justify the need for that capital to expand the corporation.

Dividend policy should be determined before you invest. If you need dividend income, you should invest in a stable corporation with a steady dividend-paying history. Fast-growth corporations need all the money they can get, and they consistently invest profits to bring about that growth.

Stockholders dissatisfied with a lack of dividends may find that the most practical alternative is to sell their shares and reinvest in a corporation that does pay dividends.

1.14   KNOW YOUR LIABILITY AS A DIRECTOR

Q. *I have recently been asked to join the board of directors of a large corporation. Considering the number of lawsuits brought against directors by stockholders, I am concerned about my own liability. What errors in judgment on my part would create liability?*

A. The first step you should take is to be certain that you have adequate insurance. Your corporation's bylaws should provide for "indemnification" to officers and directors, but to obtain reimbursement, you have to show that you acted in "good faith" and in the best interests of the corporation. I consider the indemnity clause to be inadequate protection, and that's why I suggest that you insist on a separate, corporation-paid insurance policy. Most cases against directors involve one or more of the following claims.

1. *Negligence*: This is an allegation that the directors did not use reasonable care in overseeing the affairs of the corporation. To avoid that allegation, you must give the affairs of the corporation your full fiduciary attention. Question the acts of management; demand all the information for rational decisions; require bonds for the officers; and always justify any decision you make by asking, "Is it really in the best interests of the stockholders?" If you believe directors' action is not in the stockholders' best interests, have the minutes reflect your dissent. It can protect you later.

2. *Conflicts of interest*: Always disclose your affiliation with any transaction that even appears to be a conflict of interest. Have the minutes state your disclosure and then abstain from voting on the issue.

3. *Insider profits*: If you profit by taking advantage of information about the corporation that only the directors know about and buy corporate shares before the information is disclosed to outside investors, you can be liable for all profits.

Don't buy shares until after the trading public has the same information you have.

4. *Illegal voting*: Voting dividends illegally can be another problem area. Always pay dividends from surplus and make certain that the corporate attorney and accountants certify legality.

5. *Repurchase of shares*: The repurchase by a corporation of its own shares can impose liability, as it's an extremely complex area of law. Counsel's opinion should always be obtained.

Your best protection is the confidence you have in the management of the corporation. Investigate the officers and the other directors. Check their reputations and "track records." Directors most commonly have trouble when they allow officers of questionable competence or honesty to remain in office and don't take the necessary steps to safeguard the stockholders' interests.

1.15 THE DANGER OF ISSUING A STOCK BONUS

Q. *Our corporation manufactures furniture, and until now all the shares have been held by members of our family. In prior years, we have given key employees cash bonuses, but this year we plan to give certain top-echelon employees stock bonuses equal to 10 percent of the company. Are there any pitfalls?*

A.   There may be. What happens if one of your "stockholder employees" is fired or leaves the company? A stockholder may then have two to three percent of the company, which doesn't really provide much economic benefit. At that point, your former employee may decide the best way to get you to buy the shares back—at an exorbitant price—is to harass management. A single stockholder can play "watchdog" over the books, question every management benefit or decision, and generally become a nuisance while asserting minority stockholder rights.

That's why I generally don't support giving "outsiders" a small percentage of the shares. If you are convinced that it is the best bonus plan for you, then issue the shares with the provision that if employment is terminated for any reason, the corporation can reacquire the shares at a stated price.

The one advantage of a stock bonus is that it does not require a cash outlay by the corporation and gives the employees an increased incentive, as they are now stockholders. Most wage analysts, however, report that a token ownership interest seldom increases employee motivation and that corporate attorneys consistently report that the employees holding this small stock interest are the most troublesome stockholders of all, particularly when they are no longer employees.

1.16 YOU HAVE FEW RIGHTS AS A MINORITY STOCKHOLDER IN A CLOSELY HELD CORPORATION

Q. *I have the opportunity to invest $20,000 for 20 percent stock ownership in a small three-store hardware chain presently owned by two other stockholders. What are my legal rights?*

A. As a minority stockholder, you have the same rights as any other stockholder, but you lack the ability to control the destiny of the company or your own destiny within it. Consider what your "legal leverage" really represents.

1. You have the right to vote officers and/or directors to the extent permitted by the bylaws. You can, however, always be outvoted by your partners' vote of 80 percent of the shares. Therefore, you have virtually no independent say about the structure or management of the corporation.

2. You have the right to receive 20 percent of the dividends declared. But you're not buying AT&T stock. Chances are that dividends will never be declared, as is usually the case with small, closely held corporations. Remember that dividends are declared by the directors, whose election you will not control.

3. You have the right to receive 20 percent of all net proceeds due stockholders upon sale or liquidation of the firm. Once again, the sale or liquidation decision will be controlled by your partners.

4. You have the right to inspect books. This is a valuable right if you don't believe your partners are conducting the affairs of the corporation properly, but it only gives you a right to sue on behalf of the corporation.

Considering the few practical or meaningful rights of a minority stockholder, I usually classify it as a highly questionable investment unless you have absolute confidence in both the competence and integrity of your partners and the long-term growth of the company.

1.17 THE RIGHT OF A MINORITY STOCKHOLDER TO SUE

Q. *Three years ago I invested $30,000 for a 20 percent stock interest in a corporation that owns and operates a nursing home. The problem is that my "partner," who owns the remaining 80 percent, is the president and treasurer of the corporation, and through the board of directors, which he controls, voted himself an excessive $100,000 annual salary, a leased Mercedes, and company-paid vacations. What are my rights?*

A. In addition to the rights of a minority stockholder outlined in question 1.16, you have the right to sue on behalf of the corporation to recover any reimbursement due the corporation arising from any "wrongdoing" by an officer.

The first step is to be able to show that the president breached his fiduciary duty to the corporation by the excessive salary and fringe benefits. He clearly has the obligation to deal fairly with the corporation, but what becomes "fair" rather than a breach of duty or overt embezzlement will follow a subjective test. The burden will be on you to show that the salary is excessive or the fringe benefits inconsistent with his position or financial capabilities of the company.

If you believe his benefits are excessive, then you must make demand on the board of directors to act on behalf of the corporation to stop the abuse and bring any action to recover wrongful appropriations.

Should the directors fail or refuse to act, then you, as a minority stockholder, can file suit. Any recovery would be payable to the corporation. If you are successful, the court will probably order the corporation to pay your legal fees, but you may have to bear the costs if you don't prevail.

By bringing suit, you are enforcing the one important right that minority stockholders do have, the right to have the officers and directors operate the company for the benefit of all stockholders rather than for their own personal gain.

1.18   USING OUTSIDERS TO BREAK A STALEMATE BETWEEN PARTNERS

Q.   *My partner and I will each own 50 percent of the stock in our bakery supply corporation. We are concerned about the possibilities of a "deadlock" if we can't agree on a major business decision. Any recommendations for handling this?*

A.   This is a chronic problem. The only simple alternative is to structure the board of directors so that any disputes can be decided by an "impartial" third party.

One solution would be to appoint your attorney or accountant to the board if you both believe that this is the person to arbitrate matters on an impartial basis and without bias toward either you or your partner.

Another alternative is to have only you and your partner on the board of directors (you can add your spouses if your state requires three or more directors) so you also end up with a stalemate on the board of directors. Matters of disagreement can then be decided by binding arbitration under the American Arbitration Association rules (see question 5.4 for more information about how arbitration works).

Most disagreements will involve a dispute on operational matters. Rather than turning it into an adversary proceeding, use it as an opportunity to call in an outside consultant with expertise in the area of controversy.

You may find inexpensive assistance through SCORE, which is an association of retired executives who provide free consultation through the Small Business Administration; or by contacting professors at local business schools.

This may appear to be common sense, but partners often fail to look to a knowledgeable outside source to break a stalemate and provide the company with the expertise it needs when partners disagree.

1.19   DIVORCE—PARTNERSHIP STYLE

Q.   *For two years my partner and I have been fighting with each other over every business decision. We're now at the point where we don't even talk anymore and end up working at cross-purposes. As 50/50 owners we are deadlocked. As you would expect, I want my partner out of the business, and my partner wants to buy me out. What's the best way to extricate myself from this situation?*

A.   You can do it either the logical or the illogical way. Let's take the illogical way first.

When a business has a 50/50 ownership and the partners (or costockholders) cannot resolve their internal problems, then either partner can go into court and ask for a liquidating receiver. The receiver will then sell the business (usually at auction), pay the creditors, and give the owners whatever proceeds are left. The disadvantages are obvious: Neither you nor your partner end up with the business or obtain the true value of your share in the business. A better but still illogical solution is to sell the business for the best price. Still, this will force both of you to give up the business.

I have wrestled with this problem many times, and I'm convinced that you have only one best alternative. It calls for an "auction" between you and your partner. Here's how to handle it.

1. Define the terms of sale (down payment, length of note, interest, security, covenant not to compete). These predefined terms would apply no matter which partner prevailed.

2. Hire an auctioneer or independent party to conduct the auction.

3. Reduce your agreement to proceed under an "auction buy-out" to writing so neither party can back out.

4. The business will then be auctioned between you. The high bidder will pay the other 50 percent of the price (representing the low bidder's share). You can also simply auction your respective shares.

Two owners of a large health and beauty aid store recently structured their "divorce" just this way. It was agreed that they would each put up a $10,000 down payment and agree to a five-year payout of the balance with 15 percent interest secured by a pledge of the shares. They bid their respective shares in the auctioneer's office, and the successful bidder purchased the other partner's shares for $40,000. The other details of the sale having been agreed to, the sale became binding on both. The advantages of this method are these.

1. Each partner has equal opportunity to buy out the other.

2. Both "selling partner" (low bidder) and the "buying partner" (high bidder) will receive the agreed-upon worth of the business.

3. Neither partner can claim to have ended up with anything but "the best deal."

1.20 GUIDELINES TO FOLLOW IF YOU LOSE YOUR STOCK CERTIFICATES

Q. *I owned 6,000 shares of a large publicly held corporation listed on the New York Stock Exchange. Am I entitled to new stock certificates to replace the ones I lost?*

A. You are entitled to new certificates, but the corporation has the right to impose certain requirements as a condition for their issue. These include the following.

1. Notice of the lost certificate must be given to the corporation (or its transfer agent) before the corporation has been notified that the stock has been sold to a "bona fide" purchaser. As a practical matter the security would have to be in "bearer" form, as otherwise the holder of the security could not be a bona fide "buyer" and acceptance of ownership by the corporation would create liability for the corporation.

2. Most corporations require that you post an indemnity bond to indemnify the corporation in the event that your lost stock does end up in the hands of a bona fide buyer. The corporation can demand a bond equal to the present value of the shares.

3. An affidavit of lost stock certificates will probably be required. You will have to state under oath that you lost the certificates and cannot find them after a diligent search.

Once these procedures are followed, you should have no difficulty in obtaining replacement certificates.

CHAPTER

2

Common Pitfalls in Raising Cash

2.1 HOW TO DEAL WITH MONEY FINDERS

Q. *Our corporation needs about $300,000 in working capital to expand operations and pay some long-term debts. The Small Business Administration turned us down and so have several local banks. One firm advertising as a "money broker" indicated to us that it could find us either a lender or an investor. How do these money brokers work, and what should we pay them?*

A. Move cautiously. Money brokers are no different from other professionals. Some are worth every penny you'll pay them, and others are outright frauds living off hefty advance fees without finding their clients a dime. Here's how you can protect yourself.

1. Avoid large advance fees. Don't pay more than the out-of-pocket costs that your money finder will need. Some money finders ask for a $2,000 to $5,000 advance payable on a noncontingent basis. I don't recommend an advance in excess of $500, as you should not have to pay on a retainer basis; you should pay only for results.

2. Watch for guarantees. Trustworthy money brokers never guarantee they'll find you the funds, and you shouldn't expect them to. Once you hear a guarantee of a loan be wary: It may be the mark of a money finder trying to induce you to part with your advance.

3. Check the firm thoroughly. How long have they been in business? Who are the principals, and what are their backgrounds? Are any complaints lodged against them with the Better Business Bureau?

4. Check references. A reputable firm will give you a list of other clients for you to check. You have a right to inquire about their track record.

5. How does your money finder approach your problem? Professional firms are very selective in the clients they accept. They will want to know everything there is to know about your company before they'll commit resources to finding you capital. After a thorough analysis they'll report the likelihood of success and the type of loan and sources proposed. Making promises and a willingness to accept you as a client without that research are highly questionable practices.

6. What will your money finder do for you? Some simply mail a proposal letter to several hundred capital sources. Others will work with you in developing a workable and comprehensive business plan and present it to the few sources that are most logical for your type of business and the loan you need. Find out exactly how they will present your company and to what type of lender.

7. What type of loan can you expect? With money finders you're not dealing with conventional lenders. You may find that the loans they can obtain require interest payments of 24 to 36 percent a year. Find this out in advance so that you won't be chasing loans that are unacceptable to you.

8. Most money finders work on a sliding scale percentage. A typical agreement may provide for a five percent commission on the first $100,000 scaled down to one-half percent on a loan of one million dollars. Money finders have no standard rate, but a commission of two to three percent is average.

9. Watch hidden costs. Will you be obligated to pay for development of the business plan, mailing costs, travel, computer time, or any other fees or expenses?

10. Your money finder may want an exclusive. It's acceptable to sign an "exclusive agency" contract for 90 days, but you should retain the right to obtain your own financing in competition with the money finder.

11. Make certain the contract provides that you can reject any loan proposed and that you will not be liable for commis-

sions until the proceeds of any accepted loan are received. Never pay on acceptance of the loan because many loans do not go through. When you receive the money, the broker will receive the agreed-upon percentage.

Money brokerage is no different from any other type of brokerage service. You should pay only for results.

2.2   THE BEST WAY TO CAPITALIZE YOUR CORPORATION

Q.   *I have an opportunity to open a large sporting goods store in a nearby shopping mall. Since I have over $100,000 to invest, I won't need any bank financing. How should I document my investment? As I will be the only stockholder in the corporation, I think that I should use the $100,000 to buy all the outstanding shares in the corporation. Do you agree?*

A.   No. There's a much better way to handle your investment.

Use the "split approach." Take $10,000 and use the cash to buy all the shares. You still become the only stockholder, but you only paid less for each share. Now take the other $90,000 and loan this amount to your corporation, although even here there's a right way and wrong way.

The right way is to lend the $90,000 to a close relative or friend you trust. Have this person then lend $90,000 to the corporation. To secure the loan, the corporation will give this person a mortgage or security interest on all the assets of the corporation. As the corporation repays its loan to your friend or relative, your friend or relative can in turn pay the loan to you.

The reason for not making the loan a direct one between you and your corporation is that if your corporation ever does go into bankruptcy, the bankruptcy court may nullify your security interest and say that "arms-length" creditors should be paid before stockholders who loaned money to their own corporation. They can't say that, however, to a friend or relative who can prove that an actual business loan was transacted between you. Here are the advantages to my method.

1. If the business does go bankrupt, your friend or relative will have first claim on all the assets or their proceeds at auction up to the amount then due. Let's assume that the business does fail two years from now. At auction the assets bring $60,000. Your friend or relative would be entitled to that amount as mortgage holder and would have a priority over all other creditors.

2. Upon receiving the $60,000, your friend or relative could repay the loan to you. You would then recoup $60,000 of your investment, plus whatever else was paid on the loan.

3. If you followed your method, all the creditors would have to be paid in full before you, as a stockholder, could be reimbursed on your investment. In short, you wouldn't come first; you'd come last. Chances are that you'd never see any of your $100,000 investment.

4. Let's take the positive approach. If the business prospers, you get back $90,000 from the business (through repayment of your "indirect loan") without taxable consequence, except for the interest. Without the loan you would have to declare it as salary and pay income tax on it.

Review this recommendation carefully with your CPA and counsel. They'll be able to document the transactions properly for you. The method I recommend does work. It's the best way to protect your investment when going into business.

2.3 HOW TO AVOID PERSONAL GUARANTEES ON CORPORATE DEBTS

Q. *As an owner of a small corporation, suppliers are constantly asking me to sign guarantees in which I would become personally responsible for the debts of the corporation. On one* *hand I think the guarantees are necessary to obtain the credit the business needs and to show the supplier I have confidence in the business, but on the other I set up the corporation so that I wouldn't have to worry about personal exposure. Do you have any suggestions?*

A. This is an age-old problem and is essentially a game of bluff. It invariably comes down to whether these suppliers need you more than you need them. Here's the approach I suggest.

1. Don't consider a guarantee to a supplier unless you are certain that you can't obtain the same goods from another supplier who won't impose the guarantee demand. That's the only way to find out who is really in the stronger bargaining position.

2. Don't give a "blanket" guarantee. If you must go with a guarantee, limit it to a certain amount, or perhaps only to future deliveries (rather than past shipments).

3. Don't give guarantees on indebtedness already incurred by the corporation. How are you benefiting?

4. Don't guarantee a debt unless you are certain the business can pay the debt. Many suppliers ask for the guarantees when bills remain unpaid, and their uncertainty about the solvency of the business should give you something to consider.

5. Do offer to cut purchases to avoid the guarantee. Many suppliers will "gamble" on perhaps a $5,000 order where they'll refuse $10,000.

6. Do insist that, with any guarantee, the supplier will look first to the corporation and you will not be liable unless the corporation refuses to pay for some extended period of time.

7. Do require other partners to join in any guarantee. Business risk should be proportionate to the benefits.

8. Do give priority of payment to any supplier holding your guarantee. If the business should fail, you want these creditors paid.

9. Do offer alternative forms of business security. Many suppliers will accept a security interest (mortgage) on business assets, or a consignment sale, conditional sale, or lease/buy option in lieu of your guarantee.

10. Do use common sense. There's no substitute for good judgment.

2.4 THE RIGHT WAY TO OBLIGATE YOURSELF ON CORPORATE NOTES

Q. *Our corporation will soon borrow $150,000 from a local bank. The bank wants me personally to sign the check as a "comaker" with the corporation. I know the bank won't lend the money without my signature, but I'm wondering whether this is the right way to sign.*

A. From your viewpoint, it's the wrong way. It would be better if you endorsed the note or executed a personal guarantee.

Either way the bank will have recourse against you if your corporation doesn't pay, but my method presents an important and subtle advantage to you. When you sign as a comaker, you have joint and several liability to pay the bank. Essentially, the loan is to you and your corporation. If your corporation filed for bankruptcy and was obligated to pay more than 50 percent of the note balance, the trustee in bankruptcy can sue you to equalize the obligation. That's why you should never sign as a comaker.

When you are an endorser or guarantor, the obligation is that of the corporation. Your obligation is secondary, not primary. You will have no duty to share the liability equally with the corporation. A well-drafted endorsement or guarantee will give the bank the same protection, so you should insist upon it.

2.5 WHAT YOUR BANK CAN DISCLOSE ABOUT YOU

Q. *Without our approval a supplier phoned our bank for a credit reference and was told that we only had a $757 balance and that we often "bounced" checks. This is all true, but our position is that our bank violated the confidentiality that it owes us. Are we correct?*

A. Yes. A bank owes its depositors secrecy concerning information that it acquires in the banking relationship. To disclose a balance and a history of returned checks would violate that obligation.

Most banks will either respond on a credit check that the depositor has "favorable" or "unfavorable" banking relationships or that the depositor customarily maintains a balance in three figures (hundreds of dollars), four figures (thousands), or five figures (tens of thousands). That's one reason some businesses try to maintain at least a $10,000 balance. The bank will report it as a five-figure balance, and this can mean up to $99,999. Any information beyond that is an invasion of privacy, and even this information should only be provided once the bank verified your authority to disclose it.

Of course, the bank would be obligated to produce your bank records under a valid subpoena or IRS summons.

2.6 THE RIGHTS OF A BANK TO OFFSET FUNDS

Q. *Our corporation borrowed $30,000 from a neighborhood bank, and after two years of prompt payment we fell behind by 60 days. The problem is that without notice to me they took over $23,000 that I had on deposit in my personal name to discharge the note balance. What can I do about it?*

A. You have some investigating to do. Check the documents you signed with the bank. Banks often incorporate in their "fine print" that if you owe the bank any money in any capacity and if the obligation is in default, the bank can, without notice to you, apply your personal funds on deposit to pay the defaulted indebtedness. This is the "offset" provision. You may have signed such a provision when you first applied to the bank as a depositor or when you borrowed for the corporation.

On the assumption that you did sign an offset provision and personally guaranteed the corporate loan, I would find the bank was within its rights if your loan was in default. Your business loan must, however, be in default to the point where the bank can "call the note" and accelerate all future payments due. Since you were 60 days in arrears, you most likely were in the default period.

If these assumptions are correct, then you might try to renegotiate your loan and have the bank reinstate it on the basis that you will let them hold your funds as collateral security for the loan. You will lose the use of your money, but the business will once again be obligated to pay the note.

Should the bank refuse, then ask the bank to sell you the note on a "nonrecourse" basis instead of canceling it. In that way the business will pay you the future installments, and you will be able to take the money out of the corporation as a nontaxable "repayment of a loan," except for the interest payments.

Doing all your business with one bank is seldom good policy, as you have found out. Use one bank as a depository for your funds and some other bank from which to borrow. It's unwise to give a bank to which you owe money that convenient ability to offset.

2.7 FIVE CLAUSES IN A PROMISSORY NOTE THAT CAN GET YOU INTO TROUBLE

Q. *Our firm borrowed $30,000 from a finance company. The note was originally for five years, but because of excessive 24* *percent interest we wanted to pay it off after the first year. The finance company refuses to accept payment unless we pay the entire five years of interest. Can they enforce this?*

A. Unless your note provides that you can prepay without penalty (or anticipate payments), the finance company is within its rights. That's one clause you always want in any note you sign. Here are several other points to watch out for.

1. Make certain the interest is stated as a percentage of the unpaid balance (or simple interest). Otherwise you may be paying interest on the original loan balance.

2. Watch the default clause. Make sure the default is on specific circumstances, such as missing a payment or bankruptcy. Many lenders insert a clause stating that the note is fully due should the note holder be considered insecure. This, of course, is a subjective determination that could cause the finance company to call the note at any time.

4. Watch the penalty clause. A note may assess a late penalty of three to five percent for late payments. If you are constantly late, you will accrue monthly penalties that you may not be aware of until you go to pay off the note, and those penalties can amount to 30 to 50 percent of your existing principal balance.

5. Avoid the "confession of judgment" clause. Although not recognized in all states, it provides that if you default on the note, the note holder can enter a judgment against you, depriving you the right to contest the claim or to establish any defenses you may have.

Banks usually use a standard form for promissory notes, with reasonable provisions. Further, they do not generally agree to change their loan documents. Private lenders represent the danger. Their notes often contain these problem clauses that you must carefully guard against. On any substantial loan extended by a private lender or finance company, the documents should be carefully reviewed by your attorney before you sign.

2.8   YOUR LIABILITY WHEN SIGNING A NOTE WITH OTHERS

Q. *Several years ago my two partners and I borrowed $150,000 from a bank. The note is in default with a balance of $85,000, and the bank demands that I pay the entire balance. Since I am only one of three signatories, why shouldn't I be liable only for one-third of the debt?*

A.   You are victim of a common misapprehension. When you and your partners signed the note, you probably agreed to be "jointly and severally liable." This means that the bank can look to all of you (jointly) or any of you (severally) for the entire payment. Check the note, and you'll probably see that language, as it's common with all notes and guarantees signed by two or more obligors. If the note is silent as to your "joint and several" obligations then it will still be construed as a joint and several obligation. If, however, the note states that you are only jointly liable (which isn't likely), then you are liable for your pro rata share only.

If you do have to pay more than your pro rata share, you have the right to sue your partners for "contribution." This will enable you to obtain reimbursement for any amount you have to pay in excess of your one-third. If one of your partners should declare bankruptcy, for example, then your rights against the remaining partner would allow you to sue for payment or reimbursement for 50 percent of the debt.

Use common sense when signing a note with other coobligors. If you are the wealthiest, then you will find the burden primarily on you, and you may have little practical recourse against the other signatories. Always make certain that your coobligors can pay their proportionate shares of the debt.

2.9   YOUR RIGHT TO REVOKE A GUARANTY

Q. *Several years ago I personally guaranteed the payments due to a major supplier by my daughter's corporation. At the time the business owed only $12,000, but the debt is now in excess of $60,000. Can I revoke my guaranty?*

A.   Your liability under the guaranty would be defined by the terms of the guaranty. A guarantor does, however, always have the right to revoke a guaranty to terminate liability on indebtedness accrued after notice of termination is delivered to the creditor. The reason for this is that the creditor is forewarned that you will not be liable and can refuse to extend further credit since your guaranty would no longer be operative.

Your termination of guaranty would not affect your liability on the $60,000 presently owed, as the creditor extended credit in reliance of your guaranty. I would recommend that you send notice of termination of guaranty by registered mail to the creditor so that there would be no question of receipt.

Future payments made to the creditor should carry notations that the check is to be applied to the oldest invoices first, as the creditor could otherwise apply it to debts incurred after you terminated the guaranty, leaving the present $60,000 open on the books.

As a final step, you should consider requesting that your daughter's corporation issue a security interest to you on the assets of the corporation. If you eventually have to pay under the guaranty, you would have a "right of subrogation" (reimbursement) against the corporation. You would be in a far stronger position to obtain this reimbursement if you are in a secured position.

Your situation underscores the importance of limiting a guaranty to a specified maximum amount, particularly where you cannot control the amount of indebtedness that you may eventually be liable for under the guaranty.

2.10   THE ADVANTAGES AND DISADVANTAGES OF A FACTORING ARRANGEMENT

Q. *Accounts receivable in our manufacturing firm have reached the point that they strangle our cash flow. We are considering a factoring arrangement with a local bank and want to know the advantages and disadvantages of such an arrangement.*

A. To a large extent the value of a factoring arrangement will depend on its terms and the need for this form of financing. Corporations with liquidity would probably find the factoring costs excessive, but it may be mandatory for a thinly capitalized company that cannot afford to finance receivables internally. Some key advantages of factoring are these.

1. The seller obtains immediate payment upon sale of the account.

2. The factor undertakes the billing and collection function.

3. The factor does the credit evaluation and assumes the credit risk where the receivables are sold on a nonrecourse basis.

The disadvantages include these.

1. The factor's discount may be excessive in relation to a direct loan secured by receivables.

2. The factor may impose interest charges on overdue receivables and put the seller at a competitive disadvantage.

3. The factor may be unreasonably restrictive in approving credit, as the factor is primarily concerned with avoiding bad debts on the receivables purchased.

4. The factor may use collection practices that could destroy the goodwill between the seller and the seller's accounts.

Many business people claim that, despite a factor's discount of 8 to 12 percent, it is more economical to work under a factoring arrangement. They argue that clerical costs, bad debts, and bookkeeping all exceed the factor's discount. Still, you must assess the economics in relation to your operation.

2.11   YOUR OBLIGATIONS UNDER A CREDIT CARD PLAN

Q. *Our restaurant has been operating on a cash-only basis. We recently decided that we could increase sales by accepting such credit cards as American Express, Diners Club, Master Card, and Visa. What are our obligations under a credit card system?*

A. Your specific obligations will be spelled out in the contracts offered by the credit card companies, but the basic legal obligations are these.

1. You will have to pay a fee to participate, but this may be nominal and only cover the cost of the imprint machine.

2. Your reimbursement from the card company will be on a discounted basis. Discounts vary from 3 to 7 percent, depending upon the card. You may also find that the card company has offered your trade association members a lower group rate than is available to you as an individual; this is worth checking, as even a 1 to 2 percent savings can represent a substantial amount.

3. The card company will reimburse you either the next day (on a direct deposit basis) or within 30 days; this depends upon the card. Some firms customarily pay in 30 days but will reimburse in less time for an additional discount. Check this if cash flow is tight.

4. You must honor all valid cards, unless suspicious in nature. You may ask for identification.

5. The card company is obligated to pay you as long as you comply with its credit procedures. Most card companies pub-

lish updates of cards that should not be honored, and most require direct approval before you issue credit over a stated amount. If you violate these requirements, the card company can rightfully refuse payment.

6. You will have the obligation to use reasonable effort to retain any cards presented where the customer's charge privileges have been terminated or where the card is stolen. You are not, however, obligated to use force or undertake bodily risk to accomplish this.

7. Recent court decisions indicate that you can offer cash customers a discount and can even offer the discount to credit card customers to induce them to pay cash.

8. Customers who are dissatisfied with the goods or services you provide can refuse to pay the card company; if the card company has already paid you, it can demand repayment from you. At that point the claim would have to be handled directly between you and the customer.

CHAPTER

3

Dealing With Your Employees

3.1 WHAT EMPLOYMENT APPLICATIONS MUST NOT ASK

Q. *Our personnel department has prepared an employment application, but with the new equal rights and affirmative action programs, I am not certain that many of the questions are appropriate. What specific questions are illegal to ask?*

A. It's difficult to list specific questions, but I do know that many employers ask many questions that they may find useful for evaluation but that can nevertheless cause major legal problems.

Essentially, you should stay away from any question that directly or indirectly relates to race, national origin, religion, or sex. The problem is striking that reasonable balance between finding out what you need to know without inferring that the question is discriminatory. Here are some questions that have caused problems.

- Maiden name (it may disclose race, religion, or national origin)
- Marital status
- Number of dependents (although it can be subsequently asked for tax purposes)
- Home or automobile ownership (unless an automobile is a requisite for the position)
- Education (unless you can show a correlation between education and skills required)
- Other sources of income
- Place of birth
- Health (state law may prohibit this)

- Pregnancy
- Prior criminal record (unless necessary for security reasons)

The reason these questions are considered discriminatory is that they tend to work to the disadvantage of minority groups and women and have no accepted purpose in the hiring process.

Certain questions, such as automobile ownership, education, and prior criminal record may be permissible if you can prove a definite relationship between the question and the specific requirements for the position. For example, information about a prior criminal record may be appropriate for a person requiring a bond. Give the questions on your application a two-part test.

1. Do they tend to discriminate against minority groups or women, or do they implicitly relate to the issue of race, religion, national origin, sex, or disability?

2. Are they necessary and vital for assessing the capability of the applicant for the position?

You may find that certain questions are appropriate for certain positions but not for others. In that instance either use different applications for the various positions or delete the questions that don't relate to a particular applicant.

A final word of caution: Don't rely on standard forms available at stationery stores. Many of these forms were designed prior to the sweeping "antidiscrimination" laws and don't conform to present requirements.

3.2 PRACTICAL POINTERS BEFORE YOU OFFER AN EMPLOYMENT CONTRACT

Q. *I am about to acquire a large motel. The prior owner wants to stay on as a manager but wants a three-year employment* *contract. Do you recommend contracts for employees, and if so, what provisions can protect me?*

A. Employment contracts usually favor the employee, and that's why I discourage them when representing a business owner. Practically speaking, employees can breach the contract, and about all the employer can do is enjoin them from working for competitors for the duration of the contract; actual monetary damages are difficult to prove. Furthermore, employees can fail to perform, leaving you with the choice of either firing them and facing a lawsuit for lost earnings or putting up with their substandard performances.

Any employer considering employment contracts should insist on a termination clause wherein the employer's liability would be predetermined liquidated damages in the event of termination. With this provision you have defined your maximum exposure. Of course, the termination clause should not obligate you to pay if the termination is due to breach of agreement on nonperformance by the employee.

Here are some practical considerations to look at before signing the contract.

1. Does the employee have a solid record of performance? Strong past performance is your best indicator of future performance.

2. How long a contract will you offer? I don't recommend a contract in excess of one or two years, as it's difficult to predict your employees' career objectives or your own personnel needs beyond that.

3. Can the employee find other employment at a comparable salary? If you do terminate an agreement with an employee who finds comparable employment elsewhere, the employee will have no damages against you, and your contract will present less risk.

4. Will you retain complete flexibility in operating your company? The contract should give you sufficient flexibility in giving your employees new responsibilities as your organizational needs change.

5. Does your agreement provide for arbitration? It's the fastest and least expensive way to resolve any dispute under the agreement.

Hiring the seller of a business requires special care. Sellers working for buyers often resist changes in operation and find it difficult to face the fact that they are no longer bosses. Whether you will face that problem requires a careful assessment of the seller's ability to function as an employee. You should consider a trial period before you enter into a binding agreement and are forced to pay a "severance pay bonus" if your employee does not work out.

3.3 EMPLOYEES WHO MAY BE PAID LESS THAN MINIMUM WAGE

Q. *Can you define the employees who can earn less than minimum wage? We operate a plant with 600 employees in diverse occupations and, due to low employment in our area, we have a surplus of workers willing to work for less.*

A. Federal law has its exemptions, but each state has its own requirements, which may be more stringent. Therefore, you also should consider your state law. Federal law exempts employees who fit any of these requirements.

1. *Employees of very small businesses:* This applies only to employees of retail or service businesses grossing less than $362,500.

2. *Employees working on "tips":* If the employee earns more than $30 a month in tips, up to 40 percent of the tips can be applied to the minimum wage requirement.

3. *Apprentices:* Such employees must be enrolled in a training program for skilled employment. Check the specific regulations available from the Department of Labor to determine whether your training program complies.

4. *Full-time students:* Such employees must be employed in retail or service businesses, and you must obtain prior approval of the Department of Labor.

5. *Learners:* This provision excepts learners in office and clerical jobs. Other learners can be paid less, with prior approval of the Department of Labor.

The Wage and Hour Division of the Department of Labor can give you the specifics that apply to apprentices, students, and learners. You should get the department's approval first. Under certain circumstances handicapped persons also can be exempt, but most firms do not consider it good business to discriminate based on handicap.

If your firm is a government contractor, then you should also check the Walsh-Healey Act, the Service Contract Act, and the Davis-Bacon Act, as each sets forth specific minimum wage requirements for this category of employer.

3.4 THE RIGHT WAY TO HANDLE EMPLOYEES SUSPECTED OF THEFT

Q. *One of our employees has embezzled substantial funds from us over the past two years. We haven't confronted him yet with the evidence, but we do have two other employees who will testify that they've seen him stealing. What legal precautions must we take before we accuse him?*

A. Interrogating an employee suspected of theft requires technical training because it demands not only a thorough knowledge of legal rights but also, and perhaps of equal importance, a clear understanding of technique and psychology. My recommendation is to turn the matter over to a security firm with expertise in this matter. If you do decide to handle it yourself, follow these guidelines.

1. Question the employee in private. Never accuse an employee in the presence of a coworker, as any statement you make could be actionable as libel.

2. Don't restrain the employee. Your employee should be free to leave at any time he chooses. To hold him without his consent could create liability for false arrest or false imprisonment.

3. Question the employee in the presence of one other person on the management staff. This not only provides corroboration as to what was said but also prevents false accusations.

4. Because you are not a law enforcement agent and cannot make an arrest, you do not have to read the employee his "rights."

5. Never expressly threaten criminal prosecution if the employee refuses to confess or make restitution. This is extortion.

6. If the employee does confess, have him immediately reduce it to writing and sign it in the presence of a witness. The confession should state that it "is freely made without any threat, promise, representation, or other inducements."

7. If the employee agrees to make restitution, don't accept installment payments. Once you accept the first installment, you have elected a "civil" remedy and will probably lose your rights to proceed on a criminal complaint if the employee defaults on the balance.

8. If the employee is bonded, notify the bonding company before you question the employee.

9. If you can't obtain restitution or a satisfactory settlement, then take immediate action to prosecute by filing a criminal complaint. Other employees are aware of the situation, and your leniency can only invite further trouble.

3.5   WHO OWNS INVENTIONS DEVELOPED BY EMPLOYEES

Q.   One of our employees invented a new process for manufacturing one of the items produced by our shop. The employee claims the right to the invention; our position is that because the invention was developed during her employ with us, we should have all rights to it. What claim do we have?

A. If the employee made the invention during the course of her employment, your company would have a nonexclusive license to use the invention. You would not have to pay the employee royalties on its use, but the employee can license others to use it and can procure the patent in her own name.

On the other hand, if the employee had as part of her job description the duty to develop new processes, then the invention would belong to the company, even if the employee developed the process during nonworking hours or "off-the-premises."

Whenever you have an employee who is hired to develop new items or may in the course of employment find potential items or processes, you should insert a "patent assignment" clause in the employment agreement. This clause will define your rights to invented items and compel the employee to disclose all inventions developed during the course of employ and assign all rights to the company. Many firms do offer their employees a percentage of any royalties collected from licensing the invention; others award a flat grant or bonus as an incentive.

Considering the possibilities of valuable discoveries made by employees and the problems in relying on the general principles of law, every company should develop an equitable and binding patent policy.

3.6 HOW CONFIDENTIAL ARE EMPLOYEE RECORDS

Q. *We are often requested to provide information about our employees. We have had welfare departments ask for wage reports to verify incomes, spouses demand records to determine wages in divorce proceedings, and in one case a private* *investigator wanted to see time records of an employee in a marital investigation. We would like to cooperate, but we are not certain whether we have a right to withhold this information.*

A. Your employees' records are only between you and your employees (except for disclosures on withholding taxes, FICA, and unemployment insurance).

The safest course to follow is to give no information to anyone unless the investigating party subpoenas the records. Even then you should have your attorney check the subpoena to make certain it's valid.

You cannot be liable to any third party if you refuse to provide the information voluntarily, but your employee can claim invasion of privacy if you provide the information without employee consent or a subpoena. If you release the records with the consent of your employee, make certain the consent is in writing and adequately defines the records to be released.

3.7 STAYING CLEAR OF EQUAL PAY VIOLATIONS

Q. *Our firm pays female clerks $4.00 an hour and male clerks $5.50 an hour. The pay differential is based on the salaries we have to pay to attract qualified employees. From our experience we have found that "housewives" are generally willing to work for less than their counterpart male "heads of the households." We understand that a pay differential is legal provided the employees agree to it. Are we correct?*

A. No. You have a discriminatory wage scale based on sex, and it's an illegal practice under the Equal Employment Opportunity Act and other federal laws. In fact, your situation is precisely what the law is designed to prevent, and the fact that your female employees know about and agree to the pay differential is no defense.

Because the law provides that you must award equal pay for equal work, some employers try to get around the law by simply giving the male employees different titles, and then justifying the salary differential on the basis of the title, claiming that the work is not equal. To prevent this abuse, the government will look behind the title to determine whether the work and responsibility is the same. It's function, not title, that counts.

You can pay employees higher salaries based on experience, seniority, or performance as long as these criteria are applied equally to all employees without regard to sex, race, or religion.

Your female employees could file a grievance against you, and upon a finding of a discriminatory wage structure, the Equal Employment Opportunity Commission could award them retroactive compensation, even though they agreed to work for $4.00 an hour.

Adopt a uniform wage schedule and be certain that you can justify any wage differences on the basis of qualifications other than sex. Even a pattern of higher pay for males can be suspect and open to question the objectivity you use in assessing those qualifications.

3.8   WHO IS RESPONSIBLE FOR THEFT BY AN EMPLOYEE

Q. *As a drug wholesaler, we have several of our route drivers pick up payments from our retail accounts. We discovered that one of our drivers collected over $40,000 from customers and didn't report the collection or turn the funds over to our billing department. Do we have to credit our accounts for these embezzled payments?*

A. Yes. The general rule is that, when an employee creates a loss for which both a third party and employer are blameless, the risk of loss will fall on the employer. This makes sense when you consider that the employee was working on behalf of the employer, and the employer hired and gave the employee the authority.

Perhaps the only exception to this is the employee who had absolutely no authority and the third party (your customer) who had no reasonable basis for believing the employee had the authority to collect the funds. I would suggest that you immediately credit the accounts and follow this with some simple solutions to protect you in the future.

1. Call in a security firm to interrogate your ex-employee. They may be able to obtain a confession and obtain restitution. If not, file a larceny complaint, even if you have no reasonable expectation of recovery. It will warn your other employees you mean business.

2. Bond your employees. The bonding company will screen your employees and in any event will be liable for any future embezzlement.

3. Institute a policy requiring carbon receipts for all payments. One should be given to the account at the time of payment and the other turned into the billing department on a daily basis. Make certain your accounts know of this policy and demand a carbon receipt.

4. Shorten your billing cycle from 30 days to 7 or 15 days. Not only will this give you a better cash flow, but noncredited payments will be called to your attention sooner.

5. Encourage payment by check, unless the account is on a "*cash* on delivery" basis.

These methods can give you adequate control and/or protection from employees susceptible to temptation.

3.9 YOUR LIABILITY FOR OVERTIME PAY

Q. *We operate a small pharmacy chain. We pay our pharmacists $25,000 a year and expect them to work a 44-hour week.*

*Due to a sickness of one staff pharmacist, the alternate phar-
macist had to work 60 hours a week for two weeks and now
demands overtime pay at one and one-half times her hourly
rate for all hours in excess of 44 hours. She says that, if she
doesn't receive it, she'll go to the labor board for retroactive
pay on all previous hours worked in excess of 40 hours a week.
Does she have a good claim?*

A. The Fair Labor Standards Act and the Walsh-Healey Act
do provide that employees are entitled to overtime pay at one
and one-half times their hourly rate for all hours worked in
excess of 40 hours a week (8 hours a day when working on
government contracts).

The question is whether a pharmacist is an employee
exempt from this law. An exempt employee is one engaged
in an administrative (managerial), executive, or professional
capacity.

The labor board can make a detailed investigation into the
pharmacist's duties to determine whether she's exempt or
nonexempt. You have an argument that she's exempt by reason of her position as a pharmacist, which should be accepted
as a professional designation. Perhaps the pharmacist's responsibilities extended to general store management and supervision. This would give her a managerial or administrative
exemption. Salaries in excess of $250 a week are usually indica-
tive of exempt employees.

Assuming the labor board rules against you by finding that
she's not exempt, here's what you face.

1. You would be assessed for back pay at one and one-half
times her hourly rate for *all* hours worked in excess of 40 hours
since she started employment.

2. You would be assessed for all other pharmacists, as they
are in the same position, even though they are not complain-
ing. The labor board can compel payment, as nonexempt employees cannot waive their rights.

3. Bonuses and other cash payments would be computed for
purposes of calculating "regular" hourly rate.

Should your employee win, you will face a staggering cost. Your most practical solution is to give her a discretionary performance bonus (you're not admitting your liability, but your employee will be satisfied) and then immediately review your overtime policy. Here are the key points.

1. Try to obtain a ruling from the labor board as to which employees are exempt and nonexempt.

2. When hiring pharmacists, provide them a written job description outlining their managerial and professional responsibilities and quote their salary at $25,000 per year, regardless of hours worked. The job description should also cite that the pharmacists are exempt and are not entitled to overtime pay (this is not necessarily binding, but it is evidence of the intended character of employment).

3. Make certain that nonexempt employees do not work more than 40 hours a week unless you are willing to pay the overtime rate.

4. Don't average the work week (36 hours one week and 44 hours the next). The 44-hour week is still considered an overtime week and can't be counterbalanced by shorter work weeks.

5. Don't give employees days off to be made up in later weeks if the time will bring them over 40 hours. You can be liable for the overtime. If an employee takes a day off, either pay or "dock" the employee, but don't allow make-up time.

Contrary to what you may believe, the law does not require "extra" pay for weekends, holidays, or hours in excess of 8 a day (providing you're not working on government contracts). Those benefits are common with collective bargaining agreements, but the government does not require them.

3.10   CAN YOU TERMINATE AN EMPLOYEE BECAUSE OF WAGE ATTACHMENTS

Q.   *We have an employee who is always in trouble with his creditors. At least once a month we receive a court order "garnishing" part of his wages for one creditor or another. Obviously, this creates a lot of extra work for our payroll department. Is this grounds for firing the employee?*

A.   Under federal law you can't fire an employee because one creditor garnished his wages, even if that creditor did it multiple times. With more than a single creditor's attachment you can use the garnishing as grounds to terminate as long as you adopt the same policy for all your employees.

Many personnel departments have adopted the policy that it's better to refer the employee to a "debt consolidation agency," which will help your employee work his way out of his financial problems. This will not only solve your bookkeeping headaches but will also show your employee that you do take an interest in him.

3.11   REFERENCES FOR EMPLOYEES CAN BE A SOURCE OF LIABILITY

Q.   *Three months ago we fired an employee whom we suspected of stealing money and supplies. We confronted him with the evidence, but he refused to admit his theft. The problem is that he is now seeking other employment, and prospective employers are calling for references. Do we have any liability if we tell these companies of our suspicions?*

A.   Yes. Your ex-employee can file a slander suit against you, and for you to win, you would have to prove the truth of the statement. It may be possible, but it's certainly not worth the expense and risk to find out.

On the other hand, you don't want to mislead the prospective employer by giving a good reference. Most attorneys agree that the safest course to follow is simply to say, "We will issue no reference or statement on that employee." Prospective employers will get the message, and your statement certainly couldn't be considered libelous.

I would recommend this same approach even if the employee admitted the theft.

3.12 PREVENTING EX-EMPLOYEES FROM COMPETING

Q. *Our firm services and installs vending machines in retail outlets. Several of our route sales staff recently formed their own company and are now actively competing against us by soliciting existing accounts and underbidding us on new locations. Considering that we taught them the business, we consider this unfair. Can we prevent new or existing employees from competing against us?*

A. You can only prevent competition from an ex-employee who signs a written "noncompete agreement." You have the right to impose that as a condition for hiring or continued employment.

The agreement must be specific and reasonable both as to its geographical radius and duration. The court will look at it narrowly in favor of the employee, so confine it to the area that actually represents your trading area. Your employees do have the right to earn a living as long as they are not causing you economic injury.

The agreement should specifically include any account belonging to the company during an employee's employment. You may even be able to classify your accounts, price terms, and other operational details as "trade secrets." Follow the procedure under question 8.6 to give yourself added protection. You would then be able to enjoin your ex-employees from using for their own benefit any of the "trade secret" information acquired while working for you.

Every employer with "key" employees should consider a "noncompete" agreement. Have your attorney draft a standard form that can be modified to the needs and requirements of individual employees. Strike that reasonable balance between protecting your company and allowing your ex-employees readily to find employment in their fields, and you'll have no difficulty in obtaining your employees' signatures or enforcing the agreement afterwards.

3.13   WHEN A LABOR UNION ATTEMPTS TO ORGANIZE YOUR EMPLOYEES

Q.   *We have a small plant with 150 employees. Recently, a labor union visited the plant and is now attempting to organize the employees into a "union shop." What can we do to stop the union attempt?*

A.   Calling in a labor lawyer to guide you is, of course, your first step. The checklists will, however, tell you first what you can and then what you cannot do.

1. You can let employees know the disadvantages of a union and what your bargaining position will be if they do unionize.

2. You can remind employees of the wages and benefits they now receive and how they compare to union shops.

3. You can defend yourself by replying to any distorted or misleading statements made by the union.

4. You can tell employees about their legal rights.

5. You can demand that solicitation be done during nonworking hours.

6. You can give your opinion about the union, your prior experiences with this or any other union, and the disadvantages of unionization.

7. You can notify employees that you are willing to handle employee grievances on a direct basis.

8. You can actively campaign for a "nonunion shop" and declare a stated policy against compulsory union memberships.

1. You cannot discriminate between prounion or antiunion employees on matters of lay-offs, discipline, grievances, work assignments, overtime, or shifts or otherwise enforce rules on a partial basis.

2. You cannot notify employees that you will fire or discipline them if they engage in union activity.

3. You cannot stop the union from soliciting memberships during nonworking hours.

4. You cannot attend union meetings or solicit information about union activities or undertake any covert efforts to obtain this information.

5. You cannot discourage unionization by granting wage increases or benefits, unless scheduled prior to the union activity.

6. You cannot inquire as to the employee's intention to vote.

7. You cannot offer benefits or incentives if the employees agree to vote "no union."

8. You cannot state that you will refuse to recognize or deal with the union.

9. You cannot grant financial or legal support to employees opposed to a union.

10. You cannot alter policy to terminate, transfer, or reassign an employee because of union activity.

11. You cannot directly or indirectly threaten or coerce an employee.

12. You cannot represent that unionization will terminate present benefits or overtime assignments.

13. You cannot start or encourage an antiunion petition or circular.

14. You cannot visit the homes of employees to encourage union rejection.

15. You cannot inquire about union affiliation or tendency to support a union when hiring.

16. You cannot threaten to "go out of business" if the union drive is successful.

No clear line can be drawn between some of the "dos" and "don'ts." That's one reason why you will need expert legal assistance to map out your antiunion strategy. Should you violate a labor rule, the union can charge you with an unfair labor practice, and the National Labor Relations Board can impose strict sanctions and even order a new vote.

3.14 PROVEN STEPS THAT CAN KEEP A UNION OUT

Q. *Our employees earn top salary and have an excellent fringe benefit package. Nevertheless, they are constantly being solicited by union organizers, and at this point I believe sentiment among our employees is prounion. What more can a union offer them?*

A. According to labor lawyers and union organizers, wages and fringe benefits are seldom the prime issues when employees consider a union. They suggest the following as the major reasons employees vote for a union.

1. *No grievance procedure:* Employees have grievances that cannot easily be communicated to management. They look at a union as the vehicle to communicate and arbitrate those grievances.

2. *Substandard working conditions:* Employees want more than a paycheck. High on their list of grievances are working conditions.

3. *Job security:* As employees achieve seniority, they want a certain job security. Often, seniority on lay-offs is preempted by affirmative action requirements. Unions are excellent at "selling" the issue of seniority rights and job security.

4. *Discrimination and uneven treatment:* Employees tend to measure working conditions by comparing their treatment to that granted to other employees. Disparity in pay, working conditions, assignments, and other forms of favoritism bring about significant employee unrest and make the union that offers equality a welcomed participant.

Many companies offer low pay and mediocre benefits, as do many entire industries whose employees consistently refuse to unionize. Usually, they believe that they are being fairly treated and that, should grievances arise, they can communicate and resolve them.

Focus on your own operation. You may have been looking at all the wrong factors in assessing your employees' potential to unionize.

3.15 THE BEST ARGUMENTS AGAINST A UNION

Q. *We are engaged in a long and costly battle with a local union attempting to organize our printing plant. What anti-union arguments can we make?*

A. Before we start with some of the positive points that have proved successful, remember that you can't argue that the employees will lose any existing rights if they do organize. That's an "unfair labor practice." Turn to question 3.13, and you'll find other restrictions.

What you do want to tell your employees are some of the disadvantages of a union, and it's important that you do tell them, for many employees have no prior experience with a union, and of course the union is only selling them on the positive points. The most persuasive arguments are these.

1. Wages and benefits are competitive (if this is true). Point out how your salary and fringe benefit packages compare to union shops in your locality and industry. Unions often promise more than they can deliver, and giving your employees a candid view of what they have achieved in other situations may be your best argument.

2. With unionization, promotion will be based almost entirely on seniority, not on performance. The employee can't benefit from excellent performance.

3. Opportunity to deal with the employees on an individual basis will be limited, as you will have to treat all employees by the same rules and can't bend them to fit their individual needs.

Essentially, the shrewd employer convinces employees that each individual's needs and future can be better served by not belonging to a union. That's always the message. How you say it is a matter that should be decided by your labor counsel.

3.16 CAN A UNION BE SUED IF IT WRONGFULLY CALLS FOR A STRIKE

Q. *A labor union representing 400 of our employees recently called for an illegal "wildcat" strike of its members. This forced our plant to shut down for six weeks with a loss to us of over $1,500,000. Is the union liable?*

A. A union engaging in an illegal strike can be held liable for the damages sustained by the employer.

All but three states now recognize the union as an entity capable of being sued. In the past, the courts have held that a union is an unincorporated association and therefore not an entity subject to suit, but this has changed under more recent decisions.

3.17 WHAT ARE THE RIGHTS OF MY EMPLOYEES UNDER AN ERISA PLAN

Q. *Our firm is planning to start an employer-sponsored pension plan under the Employment Retirement and Income Security Act (ERISA). What rights do my employees have under the program?*

A. ERISA standards are both complex and comprehensive. Therefore, every employer should review the plan carefully with a pension consultant. The major points required by ERISA are these.

1. Participation in the plan must commence within one year of employment unless 100 percent "vesting" is immediate. An individual's plan is "vested" when contributions become credited to an individual employee's account.

2. Partial vesting must begin by no later than 10 years of employment, and full vesting by no later than 15 years.

3. Credits for current service of employees must be fully funded.

4. Funding of credits for past service, or for service of those employed before the plan was established, must be completed within 30 years for single-employer plans.

5. You will have the obligation to provide both the employees and the secretary of labor with certain information relative to the administration of the plan.

Benefits under the plan are guaranteed by the Pension Benefit Guaranty Corporation, which is funded by a small premium paid by the pension plan for each employee.

3.18   YOUR RIGHT TO FIRE EMPLOYEES

Q.   *We have an employee who is nonproductive and destroys morale in the plant. We understand that, if we arbitrarily fire her, she may be able to force reinstatement and back pay. Is this possible?*

A.   The answer isn't as simple as it would be years ago, when either an employer or employee could terminate employment for any reason or no reason at all.

Although most courts and agencies still recognize the rights of an employer to terminate for good cause, they are becoming equally sensitive to the rights of employees who are wrongfully terminated. A few cases have ordered reinstatement and back pay when the employee successfully charged either discrimination or "bad faith" as the reason for termination. Most of these cases dealt with termination due to race, religion, sex, or resistance to sexual harrassment. The right way to handle the situation is carefully to document your case.

1. Give written notice of your dissatisfaction with her performance and provide an opportunity to correct work habits.

2. Confrontations with the employee should be witnessed by another employee with supervisory responsibility.

3. Document your case with supporting evidence, productivity reports, correspondence, and complaints from other employees or customers.

Once you believe you can show justifiable reason for the termination, don't hestitate. If your judgment is to be challenged, it may as well come sooner rather than later.

3.19   CAN A MINORITY STOCKHOLDER BE FIRED

Q. *We have three costockholders in our corporation, each owning one-third of the outstanding shares. The three of us comprise the board of directors. The problem is that one of the partners doesn't justify continued employment, and my other partner and I want to fire him as an employee. Can we?*

A.   The law is not clear on this point. Generally, being a stockholder does not in itself give that stockholder a right of employment. Otherwise, for example, you would only have to buy shares in GM and then show up at the personnel office.

Some courts, however, have recently held that a stockholder in a small closely held corporation, who invested on the understanding that he or she will be a "working partner," may have what the law calls "an agency coupled with an interest." This type of employment cannot be terminated and can legally compel continued employment.

The courts ordinarily will not require continuity in a position that your "employee" is incapable of handling or a salary in excess of his worth to the corporation. Given the uncertainty of this case, the most practical alternative is to see whether his interest in the business can be purchased.

Stockholders investing in corporations with the understanding that they will be employed by their respective corporations should all have the terms and conditions of employment reduced to agreements. The objective should always be to isolate the relationship of stockholder from that of employee. Treat each as a completely separate relationship and have each stand on its own. Any other policy will only invite litigation.

3.20 AVOIDING CHARGES OF DISCRIMINATORY TERMINATIONS

Q. *Because of economic conditions and slumping sales, our garment factory will have to reduce our staff by about 20 percent. This will result in our laying off over 50 employees. Needless to say, our employees are upset about this, and we want to avoid any allegation that the terminations were discriminatory. What guidelines should we follow?*

A. For each employee about to receive the "pink slip" ask yourself these two questions.

1. If he or she is a member of a minority group, can you support your reason for termination on a sound and logical business basis?

2. How does this employee compare or measure up against nonminority employees you intend to retain?

The overriding consideration is your ability to prove that discharged minorities did not experience discrimination but were selected for discharge on the same criteria as the nonminority employees. These are some specific cautions to observe.

1. *Older employees:* The Age Discrimination in Employment Act protects employees between the ages of 40 and 70. You can terminate these employees for good business reasons but not on the basis of age. Be careful in terminating these employees that you can justify your action on the basis of productivity and performance. Never suggest age or aged-induced poor performance as a reason for discharge.

2. *Health:* Federal law does not protect the disabled employee, but most states have laws that do. You can terminate for health reasons if there is a direct relation between failing health and performance, but not otherwise.

Pregnancy cases still cause confusion. You cannot discharge a female for reasons of pregnancy alone. Pregnant women have a right to work until they decide to take a maternity leave. While they're on maternity leave, they are entitled to the same benefits as any other person on disability leave.

Once you have determined who will be discharged, conduct a quick statistical test. Is the percentage of minority or protected employees being discharged substantially greater than their percentage of your total labor pool? If so, you may have inadvertently selected employees for termination improperly and will have some difficult explaining to do if a discrimination suit is filed against you.

A recent Supreme Court decision held that an employer can retain employees on the basis of seniority and can terminate on a "last hired-first fired" basis, even if a disproportionately large number of the most recently hired employees were members of minority groups. With this decision, lay-offs based entirely on seniority would be legal and would protect you from charges of discrimination.

CHAPTER
4

Before You Sign Your Lease

4.1 THE BEST WAYS TO REDUCE LIABILITY ON A LEASE

Q. *What provisions can we put in our lease to reduce our exposure? We are negotiating for space in a new shopping center, and the rent is high. Because the shopping center doesn't have a track record, we are concerned about our liability if the location doesn't work out.*

A. A lease can represent the largest liability facing any business owner. Here are the techniques I recommend to give you minimum risk.

1. Have your corporation sign the lease. This will keep you free from personal liability. Many business owners sign their leases as individuals and then incorporate, assigning the leases to their corporation. This is a mistake, as the owner, being the original lessee, is still bound on the lease.

2. Avoid guaranteeing the lease. Of course, this is a negotiable point, and lessors frequently demand personal guarantees for nonrated corporate tenants. If you must guarantee the lease, try to limit your liability to a fixed amount.

3. Divide your lease into options. Instead of a 10-year lease, negotiate for a 2-year lease with options to renew for 3 and then 5 years more. If the business goes, you will still have the benefit of 10 years, but your liability is reduced to the unexpired option period.

4. Assignment of lease rights is an important point. The location may not be right for you but may be perfect for another type of tenant. Once you have the right to assign, you can at least try to find that replacement tenant.

5. Make your lease dependent upon continued tenancy by the large "anchor" tenants. This is an important point for small

tenants in a shopping center. Have your lease provide that, if the "supermarket" or "department store" tenants terminate their leases and their premises remain vacant in excess of three months, then you have the right to terminate your lease.

6. Purchase lease insurance; some insurance companies do insure leases. Essentially, they guarantee a tenant's obligations. The premiums are expensive, but the insurance can pass the risk of loss from you to the insurance company should you have to terminate your lease.

Bear in mind that, even if you breach the lease and do move out before your lease expires, your lessor has obligations to reduce your loss. A lessor must take reasonable steps to reduce your liability by actively seeking out new tenants. If you believe the space can be readily leased for the rent you are paying, then your risk is negligible.

4.2   WATCH FOR HIDDEN LEASE COSTS

Q. *We are negotiating a lease for a clothing store in a new mall. The lessor wants $8.00 per square foot, and although that's competitive with rentals charged by other shopping malls, we are nevertheless concerned about the hidden extras we may have to pay under the lease. What hidden charges should we watch for?*

A. Several hidden charges should be considered, and they can be substantial and perhaps even skyrocket your occupancy cost to $12 to $14 a square foot. Be on the lookout for the following.

1. *Heat and air conditioning charges:* Are these furnished under the lease, or are they your responsibility? Utility regulations ordinarily prevent a lessor from charging a tenant for electricity or gas supplied to the entire shopping center, but many still try to do this.

2. *Snow removal or parking lot maintenance:* This is a common charge but should be defined only as maintenance, not as repair. You should try to negotiate a maximum annual charge.

3. *Real estate taxes:* Most commercial leases require tenants to pay any increase of taxes, but this must also be carefully defined. Is the property subject to reevaluation, or will the town use a new assessment method? I have seen several situations in which taxes doubled or tripled shortly after a lease was signed.

4. *Tenants association:* If your mall has a tenants or merchants association, you may be required to join and pay annual dues based on a square footage assessment. Investigate this before you sign the lease.

5. *Other hidden charges:* These may include rubbish removal, security charges, excess insurance charges, and maintenance of signs. Read every line of the lease. Unless a cost item is identified as your responsibility, it becomes your lessor's. Once you know what you'll be responsible for, verify the annual costs. Add them up, and you'll have your true rent.

Check with existing tenants. They probably have leases similar to yours and can provide you their extra occupancy costs.

4.3 DOES A LESSOR HAVE TO PAY YOU INTEREST ON A LEASE SECURITY DEPOSIT

Q. *Ten years ago we signed a lease for a restaurant building and gave the landlady a $20,000 security deposit under our lease. The lease has now expired, and we believe the landlady should return to us not only the $20,000 but reasonable interest besides. Are we correct?*

A. Unless your lease or the statutes of your state require payment of interest on the security deposit, you cannot enforce your claim for interest. Many states do require interest for security deposits on leases for residential units, but in most instances the statutes do not require it in leases for business or commercial property. Tenants negotiating leases with security deposits can avoid this problem by following these guidelines.

1. Require lessors to place security deposits in separate escrow or trust accounts. In the absence of this requirement lessors can comingle and use the funds for their own purposes. Of greater danger, a lessor may go bankrupt during the term of the lease, and the creditors would have claim on the deposit. You may not be able to deduct the security deposit from your rental payments in this case unless your lease provides for this contingency.

2. Demand interest on the security deposit. The best policy is to have the lease provide that the funds will be invested in certificates of deposit at a designated bank under your tax number. You will pay the taxes on earned interest, but at least you will have the maximum return consistent with safety on a substantial investment. The lease should provide that, in the event of default, the lessor would have recourse against the principal amount (original deposit) but not against the accrued interest. You should also have the right to withdraw interest, as that's your money and above and beyond what the lessor demanded as security.

4.4   IS A LESSOR OBLIGATED TO MAKE REPAIRS TO THE BUILDING

Q. *Our warehouse is air conditioned by a roof-top air-conditioning unit that needs replacement. Because a new unit will cost over $20,000, we want the landlord to replace it. Is he obligated to do this?*

A. Your lease should spell out the landlord's obligation to repair the premises or repair or replace such equipment as heating systems, air conditioners, and roof leaks.

Most cases provide that, unless a lease specifically imposes a duty on the landlord, the obligation to provide any necessary repairs or improvements to the property rests with the tenant. One exception to this rule is a building for multiple-tenant use in which the repair is to the common premises or to equipment used by two or more tenants.

When drafting leases, even experienced attorneys often overlook the need for carefully defining the respective duties of the lessor and lessee to make repairs. Faced with a lease that is silent or ambiguous on this point, the courts routinely say that the lessor has no duty to repair.

4.5 HOW TO PROTECT YOUR LEASE WHEN THE PROPERTY IS SOLD

Q. *Five years ago we signed a 10-year lease for our warehouse. We recently found that the building was sold and the buyer wants to increase our rent from $1,500 to $2,500 a month. Doesn't our present lease protect us for the next 5 years?*

A. That will depend on your state law and whether you complied. Most states have provisions requiring a tenant with a lease term in excess of a given number of years (including option periods) to record the lease (or a notice or memorandum of lease) in the Registry of Deeds before the lease is binding on a new owner. It's likely that a lease for a 10-year term would require such a filing, as it represents a substantial encumbrance against the property.

If your state does require such a filing for a lease of 10 years, then you'll have to ascertain whether the lease or a notice of lease was recorded. If you did comply, then the buyer is bound by your lease and cannot force you to move or pay more.

Some states hold the buyer bound by the lease even without recording if the buyer had actual knowledge of the existence of the lease. If you can obtain a copy of the agreement to sell the property, you may find reference to your lease, which certainly would have placed the buyer on notice.

Leases for a duration less than that specified in your state statutes do not have to be recorded to be binding on a buyer. The best advice is to record every lease in the registry. This will bind every buyer in any jurisdiction.

4.6 HOW TO PROTECT YOUR LEASE WHEN THE PROPERTY IS FORECLOSED

Q. *The shopping center in which we are located was recently foreclosed upon, and the bank that held the mortgage bought the property at public auction. Now the bank wants to evict us and subdivide our store, although we still have three years left on our lease. Can the bank evict us?*

A. It's entirely possible. If the bank's mortgage was on file in the Registry of Deeds (or public filing office) before your lease came into existence or before you filed your lease in the registry, then your lease would be subject to the rights of all mortgagees and lienholders of public record.

Should any such mortgagee or lienholder foreclose upon the property, then any buyer of the property takes it free and clear of all liens, mortgages, and leases created after the mortgage. That being the case, the bank can treat you as a tenant at will, disregard your lease, and go to court to evict you. A tenant, however, continues to be bound after a foreclosure. If your lease was on file before the mortgage, then the mortgage was subject to your lease and, as a prior encumbrance, would be binding on the bank.

Banks and other institutional lenders ordinarily require as a condition for the loan that all existing leases be subordinated to their mortgages. This "subordination clause" means that your lease would be construed as coming after the mortgage (meaning any buyer from the bank would not be bound by the lease). That's why most commercial leases have subordination clauses stating that the lessee shall subordinate the lease to any subsequent mortgage granted to the lessor. Here are practical steps you can take to protect yourself.

1. When entering into a lease, have lenders holding a prior mortgage on the property give you a "nondisturbance" and "lease recognition" agreement. This means that upon any foreclosure by them, they and *anyone buying through them* (under foreclosure) shall agree to recognize your lease and be bound by it. That's the only way to protect yourself fully under a foreclosure.

2. Chances are that you will have to agree to subordinate your lease if you want to obtain a lease; otherwise your lessor will have a difficult time obtaining future financing. Confine your subordination, however, to only recognized banks or other institutional lenders. You want to avoid situations in which a lessor gives a relative or friend a mortgage and then has the relative or friend undertake a "friendly foreclosure" for the sole purpose of terminating some unfavorable leases.

3. If your lessor is a corporation or a realty trust, have the principal personally guarantee the lessor's covenant to grant you "quiet enjoyment" of the premises. If you are evicted because of a foreclosure, then you have suffered a "breach of quiet enjoyment." Therefore, you want to be able to challenge someone with assets.

Fortunately, most buyers of foreclosed properties are happy to keep their tenants in possession, unless the rents are too low or they have other plans for the property. But without protecting yourself, your lease may be no better than the odds that your lessor will make the next mortgage payment.

4.7   PROTECTING YOUR TENANCY FROM COMPETITORS

Q.   *Our corporation owns and operates a chain of men's shoe stores. During one of our recent lease negotiations for space in a shopping center, we asked for a "restrictive covenant" whereby the landlord would agree not to rent any other store in the center to another store engaged in a competitive business. The landlord argued that this provision would be illegal. Is he right?*

A.   Your landlord is right only if you are a major or "anchor" tenant in the shopping center.

The FTC has enacted rules that prevent a dominant tenant, such as a large discount store, supermarket, or department store, from imposing "restrictive covenants" in their own leases to prevent competitive businesses in a shopping center. The exception here is a tenant to be located within 200 feet of the dominant tenant's business. This rule exists because major tenants had such a history of asserting such control over the tenant mix of shopping centers that these were finally deemed anticompetitive situations.

No such rule exists for smaller, or "satellite," tenants. Because they don't have the power to dominate shopping centers, they can bargain for restrictive covenants. It's perfectly legal, and to convince your landlord, simply ask for a letter from the FTC.

Chances are that your landlord is only using the law as an excuse but would rather not give you the clause, as it would only reduce his flexibility in renting other stores. That's why "restrictive covenants" aren't widely used today. Lessors of prime retail space have the upper hand, and they want complete freedom to rent. You may be successful with a reasonable approach.

1. Exclude discount or department store tenants. You can't expect a lessor to turn down a large department store with a shoe department because of your small specialty shop. You

can only expect protection on what other specialty shops may carry.

2. Define the restriction to products that are truly competitive. If you sell only high-priced shoes, why prevent renting to a low-priced shoe retailer? You both sell shoes but are not after the same market.

3. Try an "escape clause" and propose that, if a competitive shoe store does move in, you'll have the right to terminate the lease with six months notice. Surprisingly, many lessors will give that alternative protection.

A survey by a leading real estate journal disclosed that fewer than 15 percent of the larger shopping malls and centers offer tenants protection from competitive tenants. And in most of these cases the protection is only granted to tobacco shops, pet stores, or prescription departments. The reality is that these are highly specialized tenants, and the likelihood of a competitive tenant moving in is small.

4.8 THE BEST WAY TO ASSIGN A NONASSIGNABLE LEASE

Q. *Our lease contains the standard clause that we "cannot assign the lease without the lessor's express written permission." The problem is that our rent is only $500 a month and has nine years to run. We now want to sell our restaurant business, but if the buyer has to negotiate a new lease or go to the landlord for permission to take over our lease, he'll undoubtedly want the $1,000 a month the location is now worth. The increased rental will, of course, depress the value of our business. Can we "force" the landlord to accept the assignment of our present lease?*

A. Your situation may not be as "bleak" as it appears. Many cases sustain the position that a lessor cannot arbitrarily or unreasonably refuse the assignment. The lessor must have a justifiable reason. If the proposed buyer contemplates operating the type of restaurant you operate and won't create any greater nuisance or impose additional costs on the landlord, then your landlord may have a difficult time showing his decision is anything but arbitrary.

Your landlord cannot reasonably argue the credit standing of the buyer, as your firm would still remain liable on the lease. The buyer, of course, will agree "to assume your obligations under the lease," but the buyer should also offer a guarantee of the lease directly to the landlord.

If you operate as a corporation, you can transfer the business by selling all the shares of stock to the buyer. This wouldn't constitute an assignment, as the same tenant—the corporation—would still remain in possession of the rented premises. This alternative has other ramifications that I explain in greater detail in question 1.3.

From my experiences the best alternative is to reason with the lessor. Faced with the alternative of either (1) a court challenge or (2) the possibility of your not selling and continuing to pay only $500 a month, the landlord may agree to an assignment with the inducement of only a slight increase.

4.9   THE RIGHT TO WITHHOLD RENTS

Q. *Our lease provides "that the lessor shall be responsible for snow plowing of the parking lot." As owners of a donut shop, we lost considerable business over the past few winters because our landlady either doesn't plow after a snowstorm or does it improperly. Can we withhold rents or deduct the amount of rent that equals our lost profits?*

A. You can't withhold rent without running the risk of having your lease terminated and yourself evicted. Cases have consistently held that a tenant's obligation to pay rent is independent of a lessor's obligations and performance under a lease.

Your remedy would be to pay the rent and then sue the landlady for breach of lease with your damages being the lost profits. If the interruption was for a sufficiently long period, you could terminate the lease under a "constructive eviction" theory, but neither that right nor this objective seems to apply to your case.

Use some common sense before you file lawsuits against your landlady. Always consider the ramifications. Ask yourself these questions.

1. When is your lease up? You may win a few dollars on the lawsuit and lose big when it comes time to negotiate a new lease.

2. Can you really prove those lost profits? You may be chasing fewer dollars than you think.

Tenants faced with minor breach of lease situations should approach the lessor collectively and attempt a practical resolution. The next time you face a snowstorm, get a few of the tenants together and suggest that the tenants will hire a snow removal firm and deduct the cost from the rent. Chances are the landlady will either go along with it or agree to fulfill the obligations of the lease. The key is collective action. One tenant is always in a weak bargaining position, but few lessors will risk a battle with all the tenants.

4.10 CAN YOU ENFORCE YOUR OPTION

Q. *My lease provides for an original term of 5 years with an option to renew for an additional 5 years "on rental terms to be agreed between landlord and tenant." The rent for the original term was $500 a month, but for the option period the landlord wants $1,200 a month. I don't think a fair rent should be more than $750. My landlord says that, because we can't agree, the option is not enforceable, and he'll evict me at the end of the original term. What can I do to enforce the option at a reasonable rent?*

A. The enforceability of your option is very questionable. With reference to older cases, the courts would not enforce an "option" on your terms, as it was too vague and the courts are not in the business of negotiating contract terms. Some recent cases have provided that such an option as yours can be enforced at a rent consistent with the established rental value of the property, even if that value cannot be agreed upon between you and the landlord. The best evidence of that rental value would be the highest rent your landlord could reasonably get from another tenant. With this approach you would essentially have a "right of first refusal" to renew the lease on those terms.

Every option, whether to renew a lease or purchase property, should have a preagreed and defined figure or a method for arriving at a binding value. Parties will often avoid establishing a defined price as they have no accurate way to forecast the value of a property 5 or 10 years later.

In those instances the option should be based on either a cost-of-living index calculation that will take into consideration inflationary increases, or the price should be decided by an arbitrator whose determination would be binding on both parties. Anything less is an option that is bound to cause trouble.

4.11 HOW A RIGHT OF FIRST REFUSAL CAN GIVE YOU AN OPPORTUNITY TO BUY THE PROPERTY

Q. *For the past 10 years we leased retail space in a small shopping center for our large discount apparel shop. We are negotiating a new lease and want a 5-year option to buy the shopping center. The problem is that our landlord won't agree to a 5-year option. What alternatives can you suggest?*

A. The only alternative you do have is to shorten the option period. You can, however, suggest a "right of first refusal" to start when the option period ends. Here's how it works.

If your landlord decides to sell and receives a bona fide offer, which is acceptable to him, to buy from another party, then he notifies you of the offer, and you have first opportunity to match it. If you accept on the same terms and conditions, the landlord sells to you. If you don't accept, the landlord is then free to sell to whoever made the original offer.

Why shouldn't your landlord accept? You are not requiring him to sell, nor are you defining the price. The only burden on the landlord is to give you that first opportunity to buy over that of the outsider. On the other hand, you have the final opportunity to decide whether you want the property before it goes to a new landlord.

The right of first refusal must be clearly defined in the lease and in the memorandum or notice of lease you will file in the Registry of Deeds. This will prevent any breach of this provision by the lessor.

Tenants often request the right of first refusal only to find out that the lessor has already granted it to a larger or longer-term tenant. No law, however, prevents a lessor from then offering it to a second tenant if the first tenant declines.

The right of first refusal should always be demanded by a tenant who can foreseeably be interested in buying the property.

CHAPTER
5

Protecting Yourself on Common Contracts

5.1 DON'T BE VICTIMIZED BY ORAL TERMS

Q. *I signed a written agreement to buy an expensive computer system and gave a down payment of $10,000. When I signed the contract, I told the computer company I would have to make the deal conditional upon my obtaining a $30,000 loan to finance it. The computer salesperson assured me that it would be an acceptable contingency. I cannot find the financing, and now the computer company threatens to hold me to the contract. Aren't they bound by their promise?*

A. No. Oral terms and conditions, even if agreed upon, do not change a written contract. The courts will look only to the terms of the contract and can't consider other terms that are not written into the agreement. The only exceptions are situations in which either the terms are ambiguous and discussion and agreement can clarify the intent or in which one party is alleging fraud. Your attorney may try to challenge the validity of the contract on grounds of fraudulent inducement, but this will be an uphill fight.

Your experience is common. Many business people enter into written agreements and neglect to include other points that have been agreed upon, only to find that these oral promises cannot be enforced and that they'll have to proceed on the contract as written.

Make certain that *every* term, condition, promise, representation or alteration to the agreement is *in writing* and signed by both parties. The spoken word means nothing. Get it in black and white.

5.2 ESSENTIAL TERMS FOR YOUR SALES AGENT AGREEMENT

Q. *After a year's negotiation our import firm was successful in obtaining exclusive sales rights within the United States for a unique automotive diagnostic item developed by a Japanese firm. We envision the need for over 50 sales agents to sell this product for us. What essential points should we consider for the "sales agent" agreement?*

A. Few contracts offer the opportunity for disputes as do sales agent agreements. Although the agreement should be drafted by an attorney, you will have to consider several points and provide your attorney with the following information.

1. *Duration:* Is the contract for a stated time period or terminable at will? If it's for a specific time, can you terminate if the agent doesn't achieve certain sales quotas?

2. *Territory:* Can you change the territory? Can you divide it, or does the agent have it on an exclusive basis? What about sales made to a home office where deliveries will be made to units in some other agent's territory?

3. *Commissions:* How are commissions calculated? Can you change prices? How are freight costs or installation costs treated? Are commissions paid on "cash" or "quantity" discounts, or are they fixed to a unit list price? Will commissions apply to repeat orders?

4. *Right to reject orders:* Does your company have the right to reject orders without commission payments?

5. *Payment of commissions:* This is an important point. Are commissions payable upon signing the order, acceptance of the order, shipment, or payment? If they're payable on acceptance, can you "charge back" the commission if the customer doesn't pay?

6. *Exclusivity:* Can agents offer other lines, or must they work exclusively for you? If they can offer multiple lines, are there any restrictions?

7. *Expenses:* What expenses are reimbursable? (Consider auto, lodging, entertainment, local advertising, postage.) What limits or restrictions are imposed? What documentation of expenses will you require?

8. *Termination:* On what conditions can you terminate? What happens if your firm, for reasons beyond your control, can no longer handle the line? Can you terminate if you drop the line or sell your company?

9. *House accounts:* Will your company have the right to solicit orders directly? What responsibility will sales agents have in cooperating, participating, or servicing house accounts, and what compensation will they receive?

10. *Binding authority:* Will sales agents have the authority to bind the company, or will orders be subject to company approval? Order forms should make this point clear to prospective customers.

11. *Employee or independent contractor:* Are the sales agents employees or independent contractors? Make the contract specify the relationship to clarify questions of responsibility and tax withholding.

12. *Drawing account:* Will the sales agents have drawing accounts? If so, what is the extent? How will advances be repaid? Will unearned advances be repayable upon termination?

13. *Responsibility:* What responsibility will sales agents have? Are they responsible for delivery, installation, training, servicing, or processing of returned goods?

14. *Disputes:* How will disputes under the contract be handled? I recommend binding arbitration under American Arbitration Association procedures, and it should be handled in the city where the company is located.

Any sales agreement that fails to include at least these 14 essential points is one that can cause the company serious problems.

5.3 THE ESSENTIAL CLAUSES IN YOUR LETTERS OF INTENT

Q. *Our firm frequently has to act fast to reduce an agreement to writing; otherwise we stand a good chance of losing the deal. Because we don't have the time to have our attorney draw a formal agreement, we have been drafting our own "binders," or letters of intent, and have run into a few problems. How can we handle this so that we can bind the other party and still give ourselves an escape if something goes wrong?*

A. Binders or letters of intent can be the most dangerous documents you can sign. Unless they specifically say they are not binding, the courts will construe them as enforceable contracts.

The problem with a binder is that you have an enforceable contract to enter into another more formal contract. But what do you do if you can't agree on some of those important points needed for your formal contract and are still bound on the binder? Then again, perhaps you structured the deal to your disadvantage, and you will be obligated to carry out the deal on these terms.

The only instance in which you should enter into a binder or letter of intent is a situation with the necessary escape clauses. You can do this by making the agreement conditional upon the following.

- Approval of all terms and conditions by your attorney
- Inspection and verification of books and records to the satisfaction of your accountant (if applicable)
- Inspection of the building or physical plant to the satisfaction of an engineer to be selected by you (if applicable)

Once these clauses are contained in the binder, the agreement is enforceable by you, but you can avoid the transaction by claiming that one or more of these conditions has not been satisfied. Make certain that these conditions are written into the agreement. If they are only orally agreed to, it won't be considered part of the contract. Of course, you should also provide that, if the conditions are not fully satisfied, you can terminate the agreement and receive back all deposits paid.

You should consider one other practical point. Chances are that you'll have to advance a deposit or down payment when you sign the binder. Don't give the money to the other party. Have it held in escrow by an attorney or broker pending the closing of the deal. If you give the money to the other party, you may find that you have a perfectly legal right to terminate the agreement but may still have to chase the return of your deposit.

5.4 HOW ARBITRATION CAN WORK FOR YOU

Q. *As a software design firm, we frequently have disputes with our customers regarding the conformity of our product to the contract specifications. Rather than submit to long and costly litigation, we inevitably compromise the bill. Are there any methods to resolve controversies short of going to court?*

A. Arbitration may be the answer. Insert in your contract a clause stating that "in the event of any dispute regarding the contract, the matter shall be submitted to binding arbitration in accordance with the rules of the American Arbitration Association." Once you have an arbitration clause, you can have the matter decided quickly and inexpensively. Here's how it works, should a dispute arise.

1. Either you or your customers can initiate the arbitration proceeding by filing a petition for hearing with the local office of the American Arbitration Association.

2. The Association will notify the opposing party with a copy of the petition and a statement of the allegations and claim. The opposing party will then file its answer (short statement of defense) and any counterclaim.

3. The Association will then provide a list of prospective arbitrators with expertise in your field. One arbitrator will be selected that best represents your mutual choice.

4. Ordinarily a hearing will be held within two to three months. You and your opponent each present your case, much as you would in court but with less formality. You have the same right to subpoena witnesses and evidence.

5. The decision of the arbitrator is final and binding on both parties and can be enforced by the courts in the same manner as a judicial decision.

Its advantages are obvious. The total cost (fees to the Association) may be several hundred dollars (based on amount of the claim), but you can obtain a binding resolution in months, not years as typifies the court system. Another advantage is that the arbitrator, as a specialist in the subject, can bring to the case more expertise than a typical judge. To obtain more information on the arbitration process, write the local office of the American Arbitration Association.

Even if your contract does not provide for arbitration, your existing customers may agree to amend the agreement to insert this valuable provision. I recommend arbitration clauses for most contracts and use them frequently in these situations.

- Construction contracts
- Employment contracts
- Leases
- Business purchase agreements
- Sales agreements
- Consulting agreements

Arbitration is becoming a widely adopted alternative to the more costly and cumbersome court system, particularly when you want a dispute resolved quickly.

5.5 WHEN YOUR ADS MAY CREATE A BINDING OFFER

Q. *Our art gallery advertises by mailing notices of recently received artwork to customers on our mailing list. One customer, upon receipt of our ad, mailed us a check and a letter advising us to ship one of the advertised pictures. Because we already sold this particular picture, we had to refuse her order. Our customer has threatened to sue us for breach of contract, claiming our ad constituted an offer and her letter the acceptance. Can our simple ad constitute a binding offer?*

A. Generally, advertisements do not constitute an offer. They are only an "invitation to deal." Your ad can constitute a contractual offer if it appears to be an offer to a specific customer. The test is whether the customer could reasonably believe she is the only one receiving the offer.

If you mimeograph or print your circular, the reasonable person would know that it's a general advertisement rather than a specific offer directed only to her or to him.

Had the circular been processed on a word processor to take the form of a personal letter, then your customer may believe she is the recipient of a direct offer rather than a general ad.

Even a document that is clearly an ad can cause problems if you use the wrong choice of words. A statement of "quantity available" has been construed by some courts as obligating the merchant to sell that quantity on its advertised terms to the first customers who show up on a "first come–first served basis."

Another troublesome area is an absolute promise in your ad. For example, if your ad promises to pay $1,000 for a particular painting, you would be obligated to pay if a customer complied with the ad and brought in the painting.

To avoid legal problems with your ads, adopt these procedures.

1. If your ad resembles a personal letter or invitation, then use the word "advertisement" or other language showing that the same circular is being mailed to all customers.

2. Don't use personal letters with your circulars. That makes them appear to be direct offers rather than ads.

3. Indicate in your ad that "quantities are limited" and are subject to "prior sale or withdrawal."

4. If you advertise for the purchase of a particular item, make it conditional. Use language such as "acceptance subject to inspection and approval of quality and condition."

5.6 WHEN TO EFFECTIVELY USE THE AGREEMENT NOT TO COMPETE

Q. *Under what circumstances is it appropriate to use an "agreement not to compete," and to what extent is it enforceable?*

A. These are very important agreements and should always be prepared with the help of your attorney. Properly prepared, they can give you necessary protection from competition. Here are cases in which they should be used.

1. *In buying a business:* Part of the purchase price is for "goodwill," so you will not have the seller going back into business in your area and recapturing the customers "sold" to you.

2. *In buying out the interest of a partner:* Again you want to be certain that your ex-partner can't compete against you.

3. *When hiring key employees:* You'll give them exposure to customers and "trade secrets," and you're entitled to reasonable protection upon termination.

The three major points to be negotiated in the agreement not to compete are these.

1. What activities are prohibited? This requires careful definition and should include not only business activities in which you are presently involved, but also reasonably foreseeable future activities.

2. What is your range of protection? Most agreements not to compete prohibit competitive activities within a certain radius of the business. The courts will enforce area restrictions if the bounds are necessary to protect the company. Any geographical restraints beyond that will be considered excessive and not enforceable. You can also prohibit dealing with existing customers, no matter where located.

3. The duration of the agreement must be reasonable. For a small business, 10 years seems to be an outside limit, but most covenants that I have seen are operative for 3 to 7 years.

With a properly prepared agreement not to compete, you will be able legally to restrain any violation of the agreement and recover any monetary damages you can prove.

5.7 SPECIAL RISKS IN CONTRACTING WITH MINORS

Q. *Our company recently sold a used car to a 17-year-old buyer for $4,000. After three months she informed us that the car was destroyed and that because she had no insurance, she wanted her $4,000 returned. Are we obligated to return the money?*

A. You may be. A minor has the right to rescind a contract for luxuries any time prior to reaching the age of adulthood and a reasonable period of time thereafter. The minor has to give back the purchased item, but it doesn't have to be in its original condition. Even if the car was intentionally damaged, you would have to accept it "as is."

You may be able to argue that the car represents not a "luxury" but a "necessity," as minors cannot rescind contracts for necessities although they can recoup an excess price over what's fair and reasonable. Courts have customarily classified cars as "luxuries," as they are not a required item to sustain a minor.

Another possible defense would be that the minor was emancipated, married, or living apart from her parents. Many states treat such minors as adults for purposes of establishing their liability on contracts. You will have to check your state law on this point.

The safer path to follow is not to sell any item that can conceivably be classified as a luxury to a minor. Deal only with parents or guardians and let them sell or give such items to minors. Any other policy can give you trouble.

5.8   TEN ESSENTIAL POINTS FOR YOUR ADVERTISING AGENCY AGREEMENT

Q. *After 12 years of placing our own advertising, our firm now requires the services of an advertising agency. What essential points should we negotiate in our agency agreement?*

A. The larger advertising agencies use agreements that incorporate the customary terms of the advertising industry and associations representing agencies. Even "standard" agreements, however, require resolution of the following points.

1. *Length of contract:* Most advertisers give the agency a one- or two-year agreement initially with longer renewals.

2. *Possession of assets:* Who will own the ideas, ads, slogans, and other developed work? Most agreements provide that all advertising property belongs to the advertiser but that ideas developed for presentation to a prospective advertiser remain the property of the agency unless the agency is hired.

3. *Use of credit:* Will the agency be able to pledge your credit for ads, or will it buy the space in its own name and bill you? Most agencies specify that it's the client's credit that will be pledged.

4. *Decision making:* What rights do you have over the advertising program? You should have the final say on all ads and media and on the total advertising program. An important point to remember is that, although you may have the legal control over the program, the agency is the expert, and you should give your agency the opportunity to use that expertise.

5. *Securing rights:* Who will be responsible for securing copyrights and trademarks? If it's the agency's responsibility, will you incur additional charges?

6. *Competition:* Will your agency be able to handle accounts with competitive products? Customarily, an advertiser will not allow an agency to represent a competitor, but what constitutes a competitor should be carefully defined.

7. *Advertising expenditure commitment:* Some agencies require the advertiser contractually to commit to a minimum annual advertising expenditure. You should give yourself the flexibility to reduce your expenditure by committing yourself to an expenditure 20 to 25 percent less than budgeted.

8. *Compliance with laws:* You are relying on the expertise of the agency; therefore, the agency should have the responsibility to ascertain that the ads comply with all FTC rules, to the extent that compliance can reasonably be ascertained.

9. *Billing arrangements:* Most of the agency revenue will come from media commissions, but you may have to pay the media charges through the agency. Additionally, you may have extra charges for nonmedia promotions, artwork, endorsements, testimonials, and other special services. Your agreement should list all extra charges and the billing schedule.

10. *Termination:* You may want the right to terminate in the event of a sale of the business, discontinuance of a product line, or other contingency. Your agreement should provide that property rights held by the agency shall be returned upon termination.

Many advertising agencies now use simple letters of appointment instead of long, technical agreements on the theory that the advertiser/agency agreement is highly personal and that, if a good working relationship is to exist, a formal contract will accomplish little. On the other hand, if a mutually satisfactory relationship does not occur, a formal contract cannot resolve the problems and keep the relationship intact. An informal letter of agreement can make sense if it contains the 10 essential points.

5.9 HOW TO DEAL WITH BUSINESS BROKERS

Q. *Five months ago we retained a business broker to sell our restaurant and we gave her a one-year "exclusive." Two months ago we found a buyer without the involvement of the broker, and now the broker demands a $12,000 commission. Are we liable?*

A. That depends on the type of "exclusive" you gave the broker. If the broker has an "exclusive sales" clause, then the broker would be entitled to a commission, even if you sold the business.

Had the agreement recited that it was an "exclusive agency," then the broker would be entitled to a commission if the business was sold through another broker but not if you sold it yourself. That's the one reason why you should demand an "exclusive agency" agreement; you will still have the right to sell the property on your own and avoid the commission.

Brokerage agreements should be carefully drafted to protect you. I recommend the following approaches.

1. Select a brokerage firm that can effectively market your business; otherwise you may "tie-up" your business with a broker who won't aggressively find prospective buyers, and you'll have to wait until the agreement expires before you can give it to another broker (that is, if your broker has an exclusive).

2. If you do sign an exclusive, make it an exclusive agency. To avoid ambiguity, make it clear that you can sell the business yourself without a commission.

3. Don't give an exclusive for more than three months. That's long enough for any broker to perform. Bear in mind that, if the broker does introduce a buyer within the contract period and you sell to the buyer after the contract expires, you will still be liable for commission.

4. Watch the commission clause. The standard business brokerage commission is 10 percent of the sales price, but many brokers state a minimum commission of $5,000, which would be excessively high on a small business selling for $15,000 to $20,000. You can always negotiate commissions, as they are not fixed.

5. Always have the brokerage agreement provide that "the commission is only payable upon consummation of the sale." Without this clause you are liable for the commission once the broker finds you a buyer ready, willing, and able to buy on the listing terms.

6. Make certain that your broker discloses any cobroker entitled to a commission and that you obtain adequate releases from the cobroker.

Brokerage agreements are drafted to protect the broker. You will have to insist on these inclusions if you are to have the protection you need.

5.10 KEY POINTS IN DEALING WITH FREELANCE ADVERTISERS

Q. *Our firm markets several products through mail order and direct mail. Because we are too small to hire an advertising firm, we contract work to freelancers who design ads, brochures, and mail pieces. Are there any specific provisions we need to protect us?*

A.   A simple letter of agreement must, in addition to the usual terms of payment and work to be performed, say the following.

1. The freelancer warrants that the product is his or her own work and is free from copyright infringement.

2. The freelancer assigns to you all rights to the work, and you shall have the exclusive right to copyright it.

3. Pictures, photographs, and quotations of others are accompanied by releases to protect you from invasion of privacy claims.

4. You will have the final decision as to the acceptability of any work submitted and may modify or alter it as you see fit.

5. The freelancer will indemnify you for any slander, copyright infringement, unfair competition, or invasion of privacy actions resulting from your use of the material.

6. To the best of the freelancer's knowledge, the ad complies with all governmental laws and regulations.

This last point is important. Compliance with FTC and postal regulations is very technical and requires expertise on the part of the freelancer to determine the legality of the work. Many firms engage highly creative freelancers who know how to sell a product but know little about the legal requirements for these ads.

5.11   HOW TO PROTECT YOURSELF IN A PERCENTAGE-OF-PROFITS ARRANGEMENT

Q.   *Three years ago I accepted a position to work as a manager of a restaurant. My contract provides for a salary of $25,000 and 30 percent of pretax profits. My only reason for accepting the position was the percentage-of-profits arrangement, as I earned a higher salary in my previous position. My problem* *is that the owner insists that the restaurant hasn't earned a profit since I accepted the position. How should I handle the situation?*

A. Your first step will be to call in your own accountant to check out the financial statement and your lawyer to review your contract, if you have one in writing.

Unless you have a very carefully drawn agreement, however, you may have difficulty establishing profits. The reason should be obvious. Profits in a small corporation can easily disappear with creative accounting. For example, the accountant may use an accrual instead of a cash method, can use an accelerated depreciation, or can treat stockholder advances as loans and deduct hefty interest payments. The list of profit-eradicating maneuvers is endless.

That's why you should never accept a deal in reliance on a percentage of profits. Look at the percentage aspect as a bonus.

You can take steps to protect yourself at least partially from profits that can disappear at the whim of an owner. If you have a significant stake in the profit picture, demand the following.

1. Ask for careful definition of how income, costs, and expenses will be handled. You will need your accountant to negotiate these points.

2. Request an independent accountant satisfactory to both you and the owner and insist that the accountant have independent discretion to formulate the financial statements for purposes of defining "profits" under the contract. If the owner is concerned about the tax consequences, another accountant can prepare the tax returns, which may show a lower profit as your percentage is defined by internal agreement rather than tax returns.

3. Always include in the agreement a provision granting you or your own accountant the right to inspect the books.

This advice works equally well for business sellers. I have seen many situations in which a seller sold a business with the understanding that a substantial part of the purchase price would come from an "earn out," or a percentage of future profits. Invariably, the seller receives less than expected, and expensive litigation results.

Remember that the word "profit" means nothing. You want to know how those profits will be calculated and who will do those calculations.

CHAPTER
6

Your Rights When Buying Goods

6.1 WHEN A SELLER MAY NOT BE BOUND UNDER CONTRACT

Q. *Our clothing firm contracted to buy 8,000 silk dresses from a North Carolina garment manufacturer. Two weeks ago the seller notified us that it would not be possible to deliver the dresses because of a fire in the plant. We will lose over $160,000 in lost profits because of this default. What other damages are we entitled to?*

A. You may not be entitled to any damages. The Uniform Commercial Code provides that a seller may be excused from performance if it is commercially impracticable for the seller to perform. This does not mean that performance be impossible, but it certainly requires something more than mere inconvenience or difficulty.

In my opinion a fire that prevents production would create that commercial impracticality, but this may be a question for the court to decide. Courts have routinely held that government regulations that prevent shipment excuse performance but that labor strikes do not. In the final analysis each case must stand on its own.

Faced with such a situation a seller should take the following steps to avoid liability under the contract.

1. Give immediate notice to the buyer of the inability to perform. The buyer can then cancel the contract, notify the seller that the contract must be modified to accept what goods are available, or offer to extend the date of delivery. If the buyer and seller cannot agree on a modification, the contract terminates.

2. Sellers should insert a cancellation clause within their agreements. This would give them the right to terminate the

107

contract for any stated reason (whether it would otherwise excuse performance or not). Common contingencies against which a seller can guard include casualty to the plant or goods, labor strikes, acts of God, or any other delay or inability to ship for reasons "beyond the control" of the seller.

Buyers relying on shipment should carefully review their cancellation clauses to be certain that they're not too broad. If the language is too favorable to the seller, the seller may use it to advantage to avoid a contract that would otherwise be legally obligatory.

6.2   CHECKING YOUR SUPPLIERS' WARRANTIES

Q. As a purchasing agent for a metropolitan hospital, we purchase our generic drug products on the basis of price. We notice that some manufacturers have written warranties setting forth their limitations if we are sued for product defect and in turn look to them for reimbursement. Are these warranty limitations binding on us?

A.   They are if they're reasonable. The manufacturer cannot limit liability to a patient who may sue directly, but between business people these warranties are binding.

I consider a manufacturer's warranty to be a very important item in the selection process. Here's what to watch out for.

- Warranties that require you to file claims within an unreasonably short time period
- Warranties that limit liability to a dollar amount
- Warranties that are restrictive as to the type of defect covered
- Warranties that impose unusual conditions or qualifications.

Reasonableness of a warranty within a particular field can best be established by comparisons. What are the prevailing standards within the industry? Once you've surveyed them, you'll be able to spot a manufacturer not willing reasonably to back you for a defect in the product.

You should also consider your suppliers' product liability insurance, particularly if your supplier has limited financial strength. Standard coverage would be five million dollars a claim.

6.3 YOUR RIGHTS WHEN YOU RECEIVE DEFECTIVE GOODS

Q. *We operate a chain of supermarkets. Several months ago we purchased several trailerloads of fruit from California. On arrival we noticed that about 50 percent of the product was infested. We refused to pay the $60,000 for the order because of this problem. Are we liable?*

A. This is a common problem, as from time to time every business person runs into a situation in which ordered goods are defective, in whole or in part.

What you must and must not do in such a situation is carefully spelled out in the Uniform Commercial Code, which has been adopted in all states. Here's what the code states as your rights.

1. You could have rejected the entire shipment.

2. You could accept the entire shipment (which for you was not a logical alternative, as you would have to pay for all of it).

3. You could accept the nondefective portion while rejecting the defective portion.

Now let's assume that you wanted to reject all or part of the order. Here's the step-by-step procedure to follow.

1. Notify the seller of the defect and state that you have rejected it. This notice must be given within a reasonable time period; otherwise nonnotification can be construed as acceptance. For this reason, it's important that you inspect all goods as soon as possible after delivery.

2. Request from the seller specific instructions for disposition of the rejected goods. Some sellers will instruct you to ship the goods back for credit. If the goods are perishable, the seller may instruct you to dispose of them in some other manner and to credit the proceeds to the seller, as you will obtain full credit. Let's assume in your case that the fruit was only discolored but nevertheless salable. The seller could have instructed you to sell it at the best price obtainable. You would then be obligated, upon such instruction, to act as agent for the seller to sell the fruit pursuant to any reasonable instructions as long as the seller couldn't, because of distance, do so personally.

3. If the seller does ask you to sell or dispose of the goods on the seller's behalf, then you have the right to demand indemnification for your anticipated expenses. This might include warehousing costs, shipping costs, sales expenses, and clerical costs. And you have the right to expect payment on the indemnification before you start.

4. Be reasonable once you have rejected the goods through proper notification; the seller has the right to reclaim the goods or do whatever is thought prudent to minimize losses. As long as you are reimbursed for your out-of-pocket expenses, you should follow instructions and cooperate. If you don't, you can be liable for the losses.

That's what you must do when you receive defective goods. Now let's return to your case. Did you give timely notice of rejection? Did you request instructions for disposal of the goods? If not, you may be liable for payment on the entire shipment.

6.4 WHEN GOODS DO NOT CONFORM TO SAMPLE

Q. *On the basis of a sample provided to us from a textile representative, we ordered 50 bolts of the fabric for our garment company. When the goods arrived, we found them to be a different shade and texture as compared to the sample. Can we avoid the sale?*

A. If there is a nonconformity between the sample you relied upon and the goods you received, you can avoid the sale and hold the seller liable for damages. The Uniform Commercial Code imposes the implied warranty that furnished goods will comply with the sample. You should follow these procedures.

1. Immediately notify the seller that the goods do not conform to sample and that you are rejecting them.

2. Make the goods available for return. You should, however, demand full credit on your invoice (without prejudice to your rights to sue for damages) upon redelivery to the seller.

One tactical point commonly overlooked by buyers is their failure to prove the case by not having the sample on hand. When relying on the sample, always retain both the sample and a portion of the goods shipped so that you can prove the nonconformity.

6.5 YOUR RIGHTS WHEN UNORDERED GOODS ARE RECEIVED

Q. *Our retail pharmacy frequently receives unordered merchandise from a manufacturing firm that evidently makes it a policy automatically to ship a small quantity of new products. Over the past year they shipped over $700 worth of merchandise, and now they demand payment. We would prefer to send the merchandise back for credit instead. Do we have this right?*

A. You don't have to send the merchandise back, and you don't have to pay for it either. A seller of goods cannot send you unordered merchandise and impose upon you the requirement to refuse it or, through your silence, accept and pay for it. You have the right to keep or resell the merchandise and retain the proceeds.

If the goods were mailed to you, the supplier may be in violation of postal regulations unless the package contained a conspicuous notice of these rights.

Be certain that the goods were unordered and that you didn't assent to an "automatic shipment" program that could make you liable. Some suppliers have their accounts assent to shipment when the account is established. If you did assent to automatic shipments, you will have to follow the manufacturer's policy to determine your rights, but you can stop further shipments through notification.

If you are confident that you never authorized the shipments, your best policy would be simply to notify the creditor that, because the goods were unordered, you don't intend to pay for them.

Manufacturers use this technique despite their weak legal position because most accounts don't realize their rights and either pay for or return the goods. It's also a convenient way to "force" distribution of new products, which is clearly your supplier's objective.

6.6 YOUR RIGHT TO STOP PAYMENT FOR DEFECTIVE GOODS

Q. *A supplier recently shipped $15,000 worth of artificial brick to our lumber yard. We agreed to pay for the shipment on a COD basis and issued the check when the goods were delivered. Upon inspection of the goods we found that a substantial portion is defective. Can we "stop payment" on the check?*

A. Yes. You have a bona fide reason to refuse payment. Here are the steps to follow.

1. Immediately notify the seller of the defect in the goods and say that you've stopped payment.

2. Immediately put a "stop order" on the check with your bank. A spoken order is good only for 14 days, and a written order is good only for six months unless you extend it.

3. You can keep the nondefective portion and return the rest or offer to return the entire order. In question 6.3 you'll see the steps to follow whenever you receive defective goods.

The important point is to give immediate notice of the defect and the stop payment and to offer to return the goods. With those steps taken you will not have any criminal liability under a "bad check" claim or any civil liability to pay for the goods.

Quick action is all important. Too many buyers stop payment but do not give timely notice to the seller. Thinking logically, the seller will think the worst and file for a criminal complaint or contest the buyer's rights not to pay for the merchandise.

6.7 DOES A SELLER HAVE THE RIGHT TO REMEDY AN IMPROPER SHIPMENT OF GOODS

Q. *One of our carpet manufacturers recently shipped to us the wrong items on carpeting originally ordered. The manufacturer now wants to ship us the proper order. We have had serious problems with this supplier in the past and would rather not do any more business with this company. Do we have to accept the shipment of goods we ordered, considering that the supplier had the opportunity to do it right the first time?*

A. Yes. A seller has the right to cure or remedy a defective tender of goods by making a second tender after the first has been properly rejected by the buyer because it failed to conform to the order.

If the time for making delivery under the contract has not expired, the seller only has to give you reasonable notice of his intent to reship. Even if the time for performance has expired, the supplier would have a reasonable time thereafter to notify you of intent to reship. If the original order was shipped in good faith, the supplier may legally assume this to be acceptable.

If the seller follows these steps and you refuse the goods, you can be liable to the seller to the same extent as if you refused an original shipment that did conform.

6.8 PROTECTING YOURSELF UNDER AN OUTPUT OR REQUIREMENT CONTRACT

Q. *Our firm agreed to purchase all of the oil produced by a small local refinery. In the past the refinery produced approximately 150,000 gallons a year. They now advise us that they have been able to increase production to 320,000 gallons a year, and insist that we purchase their entire output as our contract states. Can we terminate the contract if we couldn't anticipate this increased output?*

A. Probably. "Output contracts," where you agree to purchase all of a supplier's production, imply that the quantities will not be unreasonably disproportionate to prior output or to stated estimates. The same applies to reciprocal "requirement contracts" obligating you to fulfill a buyer's needs. Clearly, a quantity that more than doubled does not approximate prior output.

To prevent problems with output or requirement contracts you should follow these steps.

1. Define the minimum and maximum quantity requirements.

2. Provide for termination if the quantities do not adhere to specification.

3. Establish a price or at least establish a price tied to an independent yardstick (prevailing market price, cost plus, or maximum price increase).

4. Spell out the remedies in the event of default. This is the one recurring problem with this type of contract. When a breach occurs, the parties seldom know their legal alternatives unless the contract specifies their rights.

6.9 YOUR RIGHTS WHEN A SELLER SHIPS PARTIAL QUANTITIES

Q. *We frequently experience a "back order" problem. Suppliers will ship part of an order with notification that they are temporarily out of stock on the rest of the items. Are we obligated to accept these partial orders?*

A. When goods are ordered, it is presumed that they will be shipped in one lot, unless the contract provides to the contrary.

You may be obligated to wait for the balance of the goods, but the Uniform Commercial Code requires the buyer to give the seller reasonable opportunity to deliver the balance of the goods, and the buyer will remain bound on the contract unless the partial shipments materially impair the total contract or the value of the goods to you. As a practical matter most sellers will allow you to cancel the "back ordered" merchandise as long as it is regular stock.

If receipt of the total order in one lot is important to you, your most practical approach is to verify that your shipper is totally "in stock" on all items ordered. You can also specify on your purchase order that all items are to be delivered in one lot and that you will not be obligated to accept partial shipments or back ordered merchandise. The obligation then shifts to the seller to ascertain prior to acceptance that your order can be filled.

6.10 WHY YOU MUST AVOID THE PAYMENT BEFORE INSPECTION CLAUSE

Q. *We have received an order of carpeting on a COD basis, and the invoice is marked "payment before inspection." We paid for the goods and found the carpets defective, but the seller now has our $60,000 through our issuance of a bank letter of credit. What are our rights?*

A. The payment-before-inspection clause is common with COD, CIF, and sales on documents of title. It's commercially practical, as it enables the seller to leave the goods and collect payment and allows the buyer to check the goods after delivery.

Payment-before-inspection terms can, however, be dangerous, as the seller has your money, and the burden is now on you to sue to recover. Here are some steps you can take to protect yourself.

1. Always reserve the right to inspect before payment, as long as you can do it within a reasonable time and avoid delaying the common carrier.

2. If you can't reasonably inspect the goods before payment, then inspect as soon as possible thereafter. You may still have time to stop payment on your check.

3. Never sign a common carrier's receipt as "goods received in good condition" unless you are satisfied that the goods are acceptable. All the carrier is entitled to is acknowledgment that you received a stated number of cartons, without comment as to the condition of the contents, unless you are provided the right to inspect.

4. Pay by regular check instead of cash or certified check. It will be easier to stop payment.

In your case your attorney would have the right to go to court to enjoin the bank from honoring its letter of credit. It will be an expensive process but could save you $60,000.

6.11 YOUR RIGHTS WHEN GOODS ARE DELIVERED LATE

Q. *Several weeks ago we ordered a truckload of furniture for resale in our furniture store. Our purchase order specified that the goods were to be shipped "ASAP" (as soon as possible). We have not received the goods, and upon our calling, the manufacturer informed us that the goods would not be shipped for several more weeks. Can we cancel the order without liability because of the late delivery?*

A. You are obligated to accept the goods if shipped "when due" or within a reasonable period of time thereafter. If you refuse to accept, the seller can hold you liable for the contract price less the resale value of the goods.

The key question in your case is the determination of the date the goods were due. The term "as soon as possible" implies within a reasonable time, as is customary in the trade. For example, if you had knowledge that this was a new line of furniture and may not be ready for shipment within a few weeks, then you have acknowledged that time delay.

Late deliveries can be a problem for business people. They may have relied upon the goods' being available by a certain date for their own production or sales needs. If timely delivery is important to you, follow these procedures.

1. Designate on your purchase order or contract a date for receipt. Don't mark it date of shipment as you can still experience delay by the common carrier and still be bound on the contract.

2. If it's absolutely essential that the goods be received on the designated date and not within a reasonable time thereafter, then after the date insert the words "time is of the essence." Those words remove the right to extend delivery beyond the specified date.

3. Ask for confirmation of the order and confirmation that delivery will be on schedule.

4. Don't accept goods that are delivered late, as acceptance ratifies the late delivery.

If a seller does not ship within a time period allowed under the contract, you can sue for any reasonably foreseeable damages resulting from the breach.

CHAPTER
7

Your Rights
as a Supplier

7.1 KEY POINTS EVERY SALE SHOULD COVER

Q. *Can you recommend the essential points to be covered in ordering merchandise? Our firm is a wholesale paint and lumber dealer.*

A. Every industry has its own specific needs, and what is necessary for one type of business may not be vital for another.

The documentation of sales terms should be stated in the purchase order, invoice, or catalog or seller's order form. Together, these documents should contain the following points.

1. *Terms of payment:* Is the sale on COD or on a deferred billing basis?

2. *Interest or finance charges:* These must be carefully stated for late or extended payments.

3. *Delivery:* How will delivery be made? What is the method of delivery? Who selects the carrier and pays freight?

4. *Lot shipping:* Can goods be shipped in lots?

5. *Delivery date:* Does the agreement specify a shipping date or delivery date? If receipt of the merchandise by a specified date is important, the date for delivery should be fixed.

6. *Price:* Unless the contract specifies price, the seller can charge the prevailing price at the time of shipment.

7. *Warranties:* Express warranties should be clearly stated, as should any disclaimers or limitations of liability.

8. *Returns:* Do you have the right to return merchandise? Goods sold on a "subject to return," "sale on approval," or "consignment sale" must be set forth in the contract.

9. *Acceptance clause:* Is the order subject to confirmation or acceptance? You should require confirmation of acceptance on all purchase orders.

10. *Jurisdiction:* The sales agreement should recite the state court system that will be used to resolve claims if the seller is located in another state.

If the contract is silent about any of these points, the prior dealings between the parties will dictate the terms. For example, if goods were always sold on credit, then a buyer would have the right to expect continuation of the credit terms unless the contract specifies to the contrary.

Review every transaction to make certain that these essential points are covered in the documents between you and the seller.

7.2   YOUR RIGHTS WHEN A BUYER REFUSES TO COOPERATE

Q. *One of our customers ordered 5,000 cases of paint and specified on her purchase order that she will call and specify the assortment of colors and the carrier to be used for shipment. After repeated letters requesting further instructions, we have no reply. What are our rights?*

A. Where an agreement requires the buyer to provide further information or instruction for the seller to perform and ship and the buyer refuses to cooperate, the seller may do any of the following.

1. The seller may delay performance without incurring any liability for failure to ship or for late delivery.

2. The seller may treat the lack of cooperation as a breach of agreement, terminate the contract, and recover for lost profits.

3. The seller may proceed in a commercially reasonable manner, with the buyer obligated to accept the order as delivered.

As a practical matter you should phone to find out the problem. If you do obtain telephoned instructions to ship, you should confirm the instructions in writing.

Unless you are satisfied that the buyer will cooperate in the future, your best remedy would be to cancel the order and sue for lost profits. Shipment in a commercially reasonable manner may find you chasing the customer not only for the lost profits but also for the cost of the paint.

7.3 A SELLER'S RIGHT TO DEMAND COD PAYMENT

Q. *We recently placed an order for $40,000 worth of merchandise. The supplier phoned to tell us the date of delivery and stated that we were to have a check ready for the full $40,000. Doesn't a buyer have 30 days to pay for goods unless the contract states otherwise?*

A. No. If the contract is silent on the terms of payment, the seller has the right to demand COD payment. If you don't have your check ready, the seller can refuse delivery and hold you liable for damages.

If the seller's catalog, representative, or your own purchase order states other terms for payment, then those terms become binding.

A seller will often state that terms are COD for "nonrated" accounts and 30 days' payment for "rated" accounts, or accounts with acceptable credit. If you submit a purchase order, you are essentially leaving it to the supplier to determine whether you should be sold on COD or credit terms. A supplier who believes that your firm is not credit worthy can obligate you to buy on the COD terms.

I recommend that all purchase orders contain the terms of payment acceptable to you. If you require 30 days for payment, state those terms in the purchase order. The supplier will then have to accept the order on those credit terms or reject the purchase order.

7.4 WHEN YOU CAN COLLECT FROM A COMMON CARRIER

Q. *We shipped a carload of fabrics by railroad to our plant in New York. Upon arrival the goods were found to be damaged. We are certain the damage occurred while in transit, but we do not know how it happened. Is the railroad liable?*

A. The common carrier is subject to strict liability for damage to goods entrusted to it. Essentially, the common carrier becomes an insurer. You do not have to show negligence to recover although the carrier can always defend by claiming that the goods were defective prior to shipment.

A common carrier can also raise certain other defenses; these include the following.

1. *Act of God:* This is defined as a hurricane, blizzard, or other climactic or natural disaster that could not be reasonably foreseen with adequate protection.

2. *Fragile or perishable goods:* If the goods are susceptible to damage, the carrier will have no liability unless the carrier knew of the inherent nature of the goods. Food products and other perishables usually fall within this category.

3. *Negligence on the part of the shipper:* If a shipper negligently packed the goods, the carrier will have no responsibility for damage.

4. *Illegal shipment:* Condemnation or seizure of goods by a law enforcement agency (drugs, contraband, or goods in violation of custom laws) is not the responsibility of the common carrier.

Either the shipper or the consignee of the goods may sue the carrier for loss. The consignee may sue the carrier separately even though the contract was with the shipper.

7.5 WHEN TITLE TO GOODS AND RISK OF LOSS PASS

Q. *Our firm distributes imported wine to retailers and specialty wholesalers throughout the country. We ship under a variety of terms. When does title and risk of loss pass to the buyer under each of the common methods of shipping?*

A. Here's a useful guide to explain each method.

1. *FOB (free on board):* This means that the supplier assumes the responsibility of delivering the goods to the common carrier. Upon delivery to the carrier, title, risk of loss, and freight charges are the buyer's. If the buyer's carrier picks up the goods at the seller's place of business, title and responsibility for the good rests with the buyer from that point. This type of shipment is referred to simply as FOB, as FOB place of origin, or as FOB seller's location (or designated by seller's address). This is obviously the most advantageous method of shipment for the seller, as all risk of loss and freight costs while in transit are borne by the buyer.

2. *FOB destination (or buyer's place of business):* This specifies that the seller retains title and risk of loss until the goods are delivered to the buyer from the common carrier. The seller is also responsible for all freight costs.

3. *FAS (free alongside ship):* This specification is used when the buyer designates a particular ship to be used in transport. The seller's title and risk of loss terminate upon delivery of the goods alongside the particular ship. The buyer is responsible for freight costs and risk of loss from that point.

4. *CIF (cost, insurance, and freight):* This specifies that the buyer pays for the goods, insurance, and freight charges and

bears the risk of loss until delivery of the goods to the common carrier. The seller is responsible for the delivery of the goods to the common carrier and must arrange for the freight and take out insurance in the name of the buyer. The seller will then forward to the buyer the insurance papers, paid freight bill, bill of lading, and invoice for the goods, insurance, and freight charges, as it's the buyer who accepts title and risk of loss once the goods are placed in transit.

5. *COD (collect on delivery):* This means that the buyer does not take title or risk or loss until accepting and paying for the goods. Freight charges are incurred by the seller.

6. *Sale on approval:* This method is used when the seller and buyer agree that the buyer may use the goods for a period of time to determine whether the buyer wants to purchase them. Title and risk of loss do not pass to the buyer until the buyer actually accepts the goods. Acceptance can take several forms: payment or notification of acceptance, retention of the goods beyond the stated time period (or an unreasonable time if the contract is silent as to term), or lack of buyer notification of nonacceptance. All such acts constitute acceptance, and at that point the buyer has both title and risk of loss. To avoid ambiguity, your contract should specify a definite time for acceptance. You can also reduce risk by making certain that your insurance policy covers you for goods at a prospective buyer's location. Freight is usually the responsibility of the seller unless the contract specifies otherwise.

7. *Sale or return:* This is sometimes referred to as a "consignment sale." Upon delivery and acceptance to the buyer, the title and risk of loss pass to the buyer. The buyer is responsible for the cost and risk of return to the seller, but once the goods are placed with the carrier for return, the seller again regains title and risk.

It's important to distinguish "sale or return" from "sale on approval." If your contract does not clearly specify the character of the transaction, the courts will look to the nature of the goods for a determination. Sale on approval is characteristic of goods for the buyer's personal use, whereas sale or return implies goods intended for resale.

The method of shipment you use will generally depend on what's customary within your industry, but don't hesitate to use alternative methods that can best serve your purposes.

7.6 YOUR OBLIGATIONS ON AN ORAL CONTRACT TO BUY OR SELL GOODS

Q. *Our company ordered $2,000 worth of fabric by telephone, and two days later we called and cancelled. The supplier told us that he would sue us for breach of contract. Are we liable?*

A. Oral contracts generally are not enforceable where the contract is to buy or sell personal property with a claimed contract price in excess of $500. Here, however, are some exceptions.

1. If you had accepted all or even part of the order, then evidence of the contract obviously exists, and you are liable.

2. Goods that are custom made or made on specification are not readily resaleable, and so you are liable.

3. You are liable if your order is followed by a written confirmation, which is not contested within 10 days of receipt.

4. Finally, if you acknowledge the existence of the contract in writing (even if it's to notify the seller you won't honor the oral contract) it may be sufficient evidence of the contract to make it enforceable.

Perhaps the only argument the seller in your case could make is that the fabric was cut to your specifications. To be binding as a written contract the document must contain the description of the goods, the quantity, and the acknowledgment of the party attempting to repudiate the agreement. The court will establish a "fair price" and a "reasonable time for delivery" if the document is silent on these points.

Don't rely on oral agreements. Make certain all the important points—quantity, price, description, terms of sale, warranties, delivery date, shipping instructions, and date of order—are reduced to writing and acknowledged by both buyer and seller.

If you do order goods or receive orders for merchandise, follow these with written acknowledgments (a telegram or telex is sufficient) with all the pertinent points, and if the other party does not deny the contract within 10 days, you can assume that you have a binding contract.

This does not apply to a contract for services. Although some contracts for services can be oral, they are difficult to enforce unless they're in writing.

7.7 PROTECTING YOURSELF WHEN YOU SELL GOODS ON CONSIGNMENT

Q. *We manufacture small pewter figurines of animals and market them in a display unit featuring our entire line. Most of our distribution is through retail gift shops, which accept our line on a consignment basis. How can we protect our rights to reclaim our merchandise if a retail account should go bankrupt?*

A. You have two choices. One alternative is to place an easily seen sticker or sign on the display unit stating that it's "consignment merchandise" and the property of your company. The notice might be in the form of sticker label. It should contain your address and phone number so that you can be notified to pick up your merchandise. If you do use a sticker label, make certain it's one not easily removed.

A second method is to file financing statements with the town clerk where the retailer is located and with the secretary of state. These forms list the name of the debtor (the retailer), your name, and a description of the property. You should type on the form "consignment sale." Financing statements can be purchased at any legal stationery store and can be easily completed by your salesperson when the order is delivered. You will be required to obtain the signature of the retailer, so I suggest completion at the time of delivery. The filing fees range between $10 and $20, depending on state law.

Many firms selling consignment goods worth less than $100 to $200 report that they prefer the "label" method, as the expense and added paperwork of processing financing statements isn't cost justified, but I strongly recommend the use of financing statements if the merchandise has a value in excess of $500.

If you do not comply with at least one of these methods, you will lose your rights to reclaim the goods under an insolvency proceeding as the trustee in bankruptcy (or receiver or assignee under an assignment for the benefit of creditors) would have no knowledge of your ownership and the trustee would automatically acquire title to your goods under the insolvency.

You do not have to comply with either method to reclaim your goods from an account *before* the retailer undergoes an insolvency proceeding as long as you can show the goods are subject to consignment sale.

7.8 WHAT RETAILERS MUST DO TO GIVE CONSUMERS WARRANTY INFORMATION

Q. *Our company operates retail discount stores. We stock over 28,000 different items in 16 departments. How can we provide customers with warranty information on each product we sell?*

A. The Magnuson-Moss Warranty Act requires every retailer or seller of products covered under the act to make the written warranty terms available to prospective customers before they buy. Here are several options from which you can choose.

1. You can display the warranty next to the product or on the product package.

2. You can assemble all the warranty information and keep it in a notebook. It's recommended that you maintain one notebook for each department if you operate a store on a departmental basis.

3. You can store the warranty information on microfilm or microfiche, as long as the buyer can readily use the microfilm reader and obtain all the information.

The manufacturer, as maker of the warranty, is obligated either to provide retailers with copies of the warranty with each product or to state the warranty on stickers, tags, or labels. Signs or posters are also adequate notice of the warranty, but these are generally used only on limited warranties.

Warranty information does extend to catalog and door-to-door sales as well as to retail sales.

7.9 WHAT YOUR WARRANTIES MUST SAY UNDER THE MAGNUSON-MOSS WARRANTY ACT

Q. *As manufacturers of household appliances, we are not certain about our obligations under the Magnuson-Moss Warranty Act. How do we comply?*

A. The Magnuson-Moss Warranty Act is designed to give consumers minimum warranty protection, to increase disclosures of warranty information, and to insure performance under the warranties by giving the consumer clear remedies in the event of a product defect. It applies to all consumer products selling for more than $5.00.

Under the act, a seller has the choice of giving the customer a full warranty, a limited warranty, or no warranty at all. If the seller does provide a warranty, whether full or limited, the

warranty must state on a single document and in easily understood language, each of the following points.

- The person who can enforce the warranty and whether
  the warranty can be transferred to a subsequent buyer of
  the item
- A clear description of the products, parts, components,
  and characteristics covered and the parts excluded from
  the warranty
- What the maker of the warranty will do and what items or
  services will be paid for by the seller and the buyer
- The point at which the warranty begins, if a date is different from the date of purchase, and the duration of the
  warranty
- An explanation of how to obtain warranty service and how
  disputes may be resolved
- Any limitation on the duration of implied warranties, any
  exclusions or limitations on relief (such as consequential or
  incidental damages), and an explanation that under some
  state laws the limitation may not apply
- A statement that the consumer has certain legal rights
  under the warranty.

Additionally, the warranty must state whether it's a full or
limited warranty. A full warranty means these conditions.

1. The warrantor will repair or replace any defective part
free of charge.

2. There is no time limitation under the warranty.

3. The warranty does not exclude payment for consequential or incidental damages unless conspicuously posted.

4. If the product cannot be satisfactorily repaired, it will be
replaced.

5. The warrantor cannot impose duties on the consumer
except reasonable duties that are clearly stated.

6. The warranty does not cover damage caused by negligent
or unreasonable use.

The full warranty does not have to cover the entire product.
It may extend to only part of a product if the warranty clearly
defines the coverage.

A limited warranty may cover only parts, not labor; it may
require the consumer to return the product to the seller; it
may require the consumer to pay for shipment; or it may
impose a strict time period for warranty coverage. Any warranty that does not conform to the requirements of a full warranty will be considered a limited warranty.

You can define your own warranty terms or decide not to
have a warranty at all. That's your decision. All the act requires
is that you provide the consumer with a clear statement of
your warranty.

7.10   YOUR LIABILITY FOR PRODUCT DEFECTS

Q.   *Recently a customer complained that she became ill from
consuming a can of tomato soup purchased at our convenience
store. She claimed that the soup was analyzed and contained
a contaminant. What is our liability?*

A.   Whenever a seller of goods sells a product, the seller implicitly warrants that the product is "merchantable." A product becomes unmerchantable whenever it contains a defect
that makes it unsuitable for its intended purpose. Clearly, soup
containing a contaminant would be unmerchantable.

To recover against you, all the customer has to prove is

- That she purchased the soup from your supermarket
- That it was unmerchantable because it contained the contaminant
- That the defect (the contaminant) caused whatever injury
  she suffered.

That's what makes product liability cases so inviting to customers and so serious to manufacturers and merchants alike.

The cases are reasonably easy to prove. The customer does not have to show negligence on your part. It may be that you had no way of knowing of the defect, but nevertheless, that is not a defense.

If you are sued, you can in turn sue the manufacturer and/or wholesaler as they implicitly warranted that the soup was merchantable when they sold it to you. The customer can also directly sue the manufacturer and/or wholesaler.

Faced with a claim of product liability you should do the following.

1. Immediately notify the wholesaler and manufacturer of the claim. Reasonably timely notice of the claim is a requirement for reimbursement.

2. Notice should be given to your insurance company. It may be able to make an investigation and obtain useful information valuable in defending the case, even before a lawsuit starts.

7.11 REDUCING YOUR LIABILITY FOR DEFECTIVE PRODUCTS

Q. *As manufacturers of mufflers and exhaust systems for motorcycles and motorbikes, we recently ran into a serious problem. We shipped 10,000 units of a new model to a customer who manufactures motorcycles, and it appears that these mufflers were defective because they were improperly coated with a rust inhibitor. We offered to replace the muffler systems, but the customer is demanding not only the replacement but also the entire cost of recall and service charges incurred in mechanically installing the replacements. Wouldn't our liability be limited only to a refund or replacement of the muffler itself?*

A. No. You may be liable for all damages and costs reasonably related to your defective product, as provided in the Uniform Commercial Code.

As a manufacturer of commercial products (goods not intended for direct consumer sales) you could have disclaimed or limited your liability under the implied warranty of merchantability. For example, had your sales contract or invoice contained a disclaimer stating

In the event of any defect in the goods sold, or other breach of the implied warranty of merchantability, the liability of the seller shall be limited to either (1) replacement of the defective goods or (2) refund of the purchase price for said defective goods, and seller shall have no further liability to buyer.

This is a limited liability disclaimer, as it contractually defines the scope of your liability and removes you from the broad liability imposed upon you under the Uniform Commercial Code when your contract is silent on this point.

Every business person engaged in the sale of goods to other businesses should take this step-by-step approach.

1. Define precisely what you are willing to do if any of your goods are found defective. What costs will you bear, and what procedures do you want followed? Bear in mind that you do have to remain competitive. If you don't give a buyer reasonable recourse, it will make your product less attractive.

2. Have your attorney draft a limited warranty containing these terms. This is a highly technical area, so professional assistance is essential.

3. Insert the limited warranty on your
- Brochures and catalogs
- Purchase orders and sales agreements
- Invoices

You must announce your warranty terms *before* the customer agrees to buy from you.

4. Don't fall victim to your own terms. You will find situations in which you can legally escape extensive costs because of a limited liability warranty only to lose a valuable customer. Balance the legal aspect with sound business judgment and be prepared to make exceptions to what you are legally liable for when such exceptions are in your best business interests.

CHAPTER
8

Promoting Your Product Legally

8.1 THE RIGHT WAY TO USE TESTIMONIALS AND ENDORSEMENTS

Q. *As a publisher of textbooks, we frequently receive complimentary letters from professors and college administrators. Can we quote excerpts from these letters without approval?*

A. You can quote excerpts without approval, as long as you do not disclose the identity of the person or institution. Some advertisers simply use the person's initials, and because that does not disclose identity, no consent is required.

Of course, "blind" endorsements have limited advertising impact, and your ad would have considerably increased credibility if the endorsement disclosed the identity of the person providing it. This, however, requires consent; otherwise, it's an invasion of privacy. On any endorsement or testimonial used in promoting your product, be sure to follow these guidelines.

1. Obtain the written consent of the endorsing party.

2. Have the person approve the entire ad. The endorsing party will often authorize use of the endorsement and then rescind the consent if he or she does not approve the ad.

3. Don't quote the endorsement out of context. You can use a partial quotation, as long as the deleted portion does not materially change the context of the quoted part.

4. Fictitious endorsements claiming the approval of organizations set up by the advertiser constitute a deceptive trade practice and can be stopped by the FTC.

5. Broad assertions that the product is approved by "specialists" or "experts" without strong evidence that the product has the approval of a sufficiently large number of people who can qualify as "specialists" is also forbidden by the FTC.

6. You cannot use the picture of a person on an advertisement without that person's written consent.

8.2   WHEN YOUR COMPETITORS ARE COMPETING UNFAIRLY

Q. *A competitive muffler dealer recently adopted a name very similar to ours. In addition, the competitor's signs are almost the same distinctive shape, color, and style of lettering as our signs. We suspect that prospective customers are confused and believe they are dealing with our firm when shopping at our competitor's. What will we have to prove in court to stop this unfair competition?*

A.   The elements to prove in an unfair competition case are these.

1. You must show that your firm had prior use of the name and a distinctive sign.

2. You must show that your name and sign have an established identification, reputation, and "meaning" within your geographical market.

3. You must show that your competitor's name and sign are so similar to yours that customers may think they are dealing with you when shopping with your competitor.

Essentially, the court will look at the names and signs and consider whether a motorist may, in the few moments available to observe the sign, mistake your competitor's outlet for yours. It's a subjective test. Undoubtedly, your attorney will want:

- Evidence of the date you adopted your name and sign
- Evidence of the date your competitor adopted the other name and sign (your use must be well in advance to substantiate your claim of existing reputation and recognition)

- Pictures of the respective signs
- Evidence that customers have been confused (customers who will testify make the strongest case).

Once you prove your claim, the court may enjoin continued use of the name and/or sign by your competitor or may compel a sufficient change to erase the likelihood of confusion. In addition, you may be awarded damages for the lost profits. Some courts may even assess punitive damages if the unfair acts were intentional or deliberate.

A word of final advice: If you think you can make the case, act quickly. Many courts require timely action on your part if they are to protect you. Don't tolerate the situation for two years and then complain.

8.3   THE LEGALITY OF THE TIE-IN SALES AGREEMENT

Q.   *As a manufacturer of industrial coatings, we have found that our own brand of solvent works best in applying the coatings. We want to adopt a sales policy whereby customers must use our brand of solvent if they are to have recourse to us under our warranty. Would this provision in our sales contract be enforceable?*

A.   You are trying to create a "tie-in" sale whereby the customer, in buying one product from you (the industrial coatings), would be obligated to buy your solvent as a condition for having the benefits of your warranty protection for defects in the coating.

"Tie-in" sales are generally illegal under the federal Clayton Act, but one exception would be a demonstration that only your product (the solvent) will work adequately on your industrial coatings. If a competitor's solvent works equally well, then the only apparent purpose of your "tie-in" sale is to lessen competition, and that's what the Clayton Act is designed to prevent.

Your first step then would be to conduct adequate scientific testing to prove that only your brand of solvent works properly, or at least best, with your industrial coatings. You will need that evidence if your policy is challenged.

You may also avoid liability because you do not *require* purchase of your brand of solvent but only make its purchase a condition for your warranty protection. Most cases under the Clayton Act question its legality only when the supplier requires the customer to buy the tie-in product.

You do have the right to impose any reasonable disclaimers or limitations in your warranty. Therefore, this condition for warranty protection would in all likelihood be legal.

One factor that will be considered by the courts in reviewing your policy is your market position. Firms with dominant positions within their industries have to be extremely cautious in adopting a tie-in sales policy. Firms considering policies that require customers to buy one product as a requisite for obtaining another should immediately have such policies reviewed by their counsels.

Why not consider offering the two products as a unit? Packaging product X with product Y and selling the two together would be legal. This is one approach widely used to enhance the sales of multiple product lines without running the risk of violating the Clayton Act.

8.4 FOUR ADVANTAGES OF A FEDERAL TRADEMARK

Q. *Our firm developed a new burglar alarm system that we want to market under the trademarked name of "Sona-Alarm." Should we file a state trademark?*

A. I suggest a federal trademark. It will give you far greater protection and shouldn't cost you much more to obtain. Consider the advantages of federal registration.

1. A state trademark only protects you from infringement within your state. The federal trademark gives you national protection. You never know when you will want to expand outside your state, so why not cover every conceivable market?

2. A federal trademark prevents even the import of goods with a deceptively similar name.

3. State trademarks usually extend only to products. Federal trademarks can even be applied to services. Perhaps you will want to advertise under the "Sona-Alarm system for burglary protection." This denotes a service, and you will have the right to protection for your "Sona-Alarm Service Program" if you register a service mark.

4. With a state trademark you can only enforce your rights in state court. With a federal trademark you can enjoin infringement in the federal courts. Although both courts have essentially the same powers, I prefer the federal courts, as they are well experienced with trademark contests.

Your first step is to make certain that the name is available. Your attorney can easily do that by corresponding with a Washington, D.C., trademark attorney who can check on the availability of the name within a few days. Of course, if the name is already owned by someone else with a federal trademark on it, you still cannot obtain a state trademark.

8.5 HANDLING UNSOLICITED IDEAS

Q. As a direct mail firm with a widespread reputation for developing and marketing unique consumer items, we commonly receive unsolicited ideas. Some people will mail us the idea itself, and others will go so far as to mail us a completed sample. Our problem is that we always have products of our own under development, and we don't want to be accused of duplicating somebody else's idea.

A. For unsolicited ideas that don't interest you, follow this policy.

1. Return the letter or product to the sender immediately.

2. Accompanying it should be a form letter of your own rejecting the idea. Your letter should point out that your company is considering many ideas, and some may be comparable to that submitted.

If your company should solicit ideas for new products, then *before* the idea is submitted, have the person submitting the idea sign an agreement with the following four points.

1. The company is developing many product ideas, and the idea submitted may have already been considered or is under present consideration.

2. Compensation will be payable only if the company accepts the idea and enters into a purchase or license agreement on acceptable terms.

3. The company cannot be responsible for holding the idea confidential.

4. If the idea is not suitable, the submission (and only sample) will be returned at the expense of the submitting party.

Unfortunately, you may have instances in which you do have such a disclosure agreement and find yourself embroiled in a lawsuit involving a claim that you "pirated" the submitted idea. Your best protection in this case is to keep internal records so that you can prove that your company previously had the idea under consideration.

8.6   PROTECTING TRADE SECRETS

Q. *As a manufacturer of computer components, we have consistently run into the problem of employees' stealing our trade secrets and using them to the advantage of their new employer. In some instances prior employees have even opened their own shops and used these trade secrets in direct competition with us. How can we stop this?*

A. The first step is to see what it is that you can protect, for it may go far beyond what you have imagined.

A "trade secret" is anything used in your business and not generally or commonly known within your industry. It doesn't have to be a secret process or formula. Here's a list of items courts have held to be trade secrets subject to protection.

- Systems and processes for manufacturing or distribution, if peculiar to your business
- The design of equipment and layout
- Customers' lists and mailing lists
- Prices charged to customers and charged by vendors
- Lists of qualified vendors
- Any financial information relating to the company
- Internal memoranda, blueprints, product molds, sketches, and computer programs (unless commercially available).

Once you have defined what information is subject to protection, then you have to take reasonable steps to protect it. Courts take the position that, unless you choose to consider it a "trade secret," the courts won't treat it as such. The best approach to follow is this.

1. Compile a list (by general description) of all items you consider trade secrets.

2. Your house bulletin or hiring forms should forewarn all employees that these items are trade secrets.

3. Have each employee sign a confidential information, or "nondisclosure," agreement, stating

- That the employee acknowledges the items to be trade secrets
- That the employee will not directly or indirectly disclose or use the trade secrets for personal gain or for the gain of any other
- That upon termination of employment the employee will return any trade secrets (or copies or reproductions) in that employee's possession

- That any future employer may be advised of the existence of the nondisclosure agreement.

Your attorney can draft an appropriate nondisclosure agreement incorporating these points.

For employees occupying strategic positions within the firm, you can increase your protection by coupling the nondisclosure agreement with a noncompete provision barring the employee from going into a competitive line within a certain radius and time. Turn to question 3.12 for more information on how this works.

8.7 CAN YOU RESTRICT A DISTRIBUTOR FROM HANDLING GOODS OF A COMPETITOR

Q. *We manufacture a line of plumbing supplies and intend to expand through national distributorships. Can we legally restrict our distributors from carrying a competitive line?*

A. These arrangements may be legal if you have a rational business reason for the exclusive agreement. Here's what the FTC will consider.

1. Do you have a proper business purpose for the arrangement? For example, is exclusivity needed to ensure a market for your output? If you have adequate distribution opportunities without an exclusive agreement, your policy may be challenged.

2. Is there a trend toward concentration in the industry? If you hold a dominant share of the market, serious questions of legality will be raised.

3. Have you avoided minimum resale price provisions in your agreement, defined the distributor's territory, and

required performance by your distributor in promoting your products? These clauses must meet with the approval of the FTC.

4. How restrictive is the exclusive? Are you preventing your distributor from selling noncompetitive lines produced by a competitor? The exclusive should be narrowed to products that are in direct competition.

5. How long will the exclusive agreement run? The FTC suggests that exclusive dealing agreements shouldn't impose a restriction on a distributor for more than two or three years.

As you can see, the legality of an exclusive dealing agreement requires the careful analysis of several subjective points. You can request a ruling from the FTC on the legality of your plan before you put it into effect, and if your distributorship program is extensive, a presigning clearance may save you later problems.

8.8 WHEN YOU CAN LEGALLY DISCRIMINATE IN PRICE

Q. *Our company manufactures a line of aquarium tanks and supplies for sale to pet shops. One of our prime customers, a large department store chain that has purchased as much as $200,000 a year from us, recently advised us that it is discontinuing our line. The reason is that a competitor will sell a comparable product line at a price well below our list price. We can match the competitor's price and still make a profit, but we don't want to lower the price to our other customers. How can we handle the situation?*

A. Under the Robinson-Patman Act, one of the several "antitrust" laws, it is illegal to discriminate in price between customers at the same competitive level of distribution. There are two important exceptions. The first states that you can reduce your price to a given customer if it's necessary to maintain an account and "meet competition." This exemption seems to correspond to your situation. Here's how to handle it.

1. Ask the department store to send you a letter confirming the competitor's price and the fact that it plans to discontinue your line because of your higher price. With this documentation on hand you can prove that your reduced price was necessary to meet competition and keep the account. You will then be free of liability.

2. You can then do even better than simply "meeting" the competitor's price. You can sell at an even lower price if you can show that doing so was probably necessary to solidify the account.

The second exception to the Robinson-Patman Act is "cost justification." You have a right to pass on to your customers the savings to you resulting from quantity purchases. For example, if you can prove that you save $5.00 on an item by selling in quantities of 100 units rather than 10 units, you can then reduce your price to the 100-unit buyers by $5.00 a unit. In your case, however, you could only reduce your price to your department store account to reflect the "pass through" savings that a $200,000-a-year account represents as compared to a smaller account. Because this would obligate you to reduce your price similarly to other buyers who buy on equally proportionate terms, it could needlessly erode profit margins, and you might still end up with a price to the department store that is noncompetitive against the rival supplier.

Your best bet is to go on the basis of meeting competition, as this is the approach that gives you greatest flexibility, profit preservation, and solid documentation that you are complying with the law.

8.9 HOW TO HANDLE PROMOTIONAL ALLOWANCES LEGALLY

Q. *We have developed a new line of flashlights, and to promote it we want to offer all our larger department store and discount store customers a 10 percent display allowance. Do we have to offer the same discount to retail accounts buying our line through wholesalers and jobbers?*

A. Absolutely. Advertising, promotional, and trade allowances and discounts or incentives must be offered on equally proportionate terms to all retail outlets carrying your line, whether they buy directly or through a wholesaler.

You must extend the discount to the wholesalers, which in turn must pass it on to the retail accounts. This prevents unfair advantage to the larger retailers who can afford to buy directly and in quantity. Test your compliance with the Robinson-Patman Act.

1. Do you grant the same allowances to accounts that buy through wholesalers as to those that buy directly?

2. Do you offer the allowances to all categories of retail customers selling your product?

3. Do you reasonably advertise the availability of the allowance to *all* your accounts?

4. Do you have a reasonable alternative to your standard display for retail accounts that cannot use or merchandise your mass-merchandising display?

5. Do you offer the same proportionate allowances to all your accounts?

If you answered "no" to any of the foregoing questions, it's time to review your marketing plan. You may be out of compliance.

8.10   OBTAINING A COPYRIGHT

Q. *As a mail order firm, we are about to produce a circular to go to 50,000 prospective customers. We think the circular has an excellent design, and we want to make certain that our competitors don't copy it. Is it a complicated process to obtain a copyright?*

A.   It's very simple. All you have to do is place the notice—copyright, your company name, and the date—in a conspicuous place on the cover of your circular. You can look at the back of the title page of this or any book to see how a copyright notice appears.

You do not have to register the copyright. Although it's strongly recommended that you do file your copyrights on such substantial work as books or magazines, it's not necessary for short-life documents, such as a circular. You should, however, register the copyright before you commence any litigation for its infringement. You can obtain the required form from the U.S. Copyright Office, file it with a copy of the copyrighted material, and pay a small fee.

CHAPTER
9

Franchising Law Made Simple

9.1 BEFORE YOU SIGN A FRANCHISE AGREEMENT

Q. *I found a franchise company selling "health spa" franchises. The company is only two years old and has grown to 16 franchised units in that time. The franchisor tells me I can earn upwards of $100,000 a year on my franchise, which will cost me $75,000. What's the best way to check a franchisor so that I can have some confidence in what I'm buying?*

A. Nobody has a crystal ball to determine whether a franchise system will turn out to be another McDonald's or will fall on its face with the operators chased by the bunko squad. But you can hedge your bet with some careful investigation.

I have represented many prospective franchisees; some ended up with highly valuable businesses, and others have lost entire investments. It's such a risky business that careful and skeptical investigation is essential. Here's a checklist to follow as you go about your investigation.

1. Check with the FTC to determine whether any complaints have been filed against the franchisor. Check not only the Washington, D.C., office but with branch offices in places that the franchisor maintains a place of business. You should also check the International Franchise Association in Washington.

2. The franchisor must give you a complete "disclosure" statement before you sign the franchise agreement. This will include a background of the principals, the company, projected financial statements, start-up costs, and pending litigation. Review it thoroughly.

3. Go beyond the disclosure statement. Check the principals' backgrounds. Ask for copies of other franchisees' profit

and loss statements. Talk to suppliers and creditors. You have to go beyond the written words to get the full story.

4. Talk to existing franchisees. This is your most important safeguard. If you find that most of them say that the franchisor delivered what was promised, then you have your best assurance—their recommendation. You should select the franchisees to interview at random. Don't limit yourself to franchisees that the franchisor steers you to.

5. Have your accountant review the franchisor's financial statements. Many well-intentioned franchise systems market a sound business idea but nevertheless collapse because of fiscal problems. Make certain the franchisor can back integrity with stability.

6. Be wary of franchise offerings in which you have to put up all the cash. Although there are some excellent programs that don't offer financing, you are appreciably safer with a system in which a franchiser system matches your money with its own.

7. I don't recommend any franchise system without a two- to three-year track record. You'll pay more for the franchise than you would if you had entered on the ground floor, but your investment will be far safer.

8. See whether you can work at one of the franchised units for two to three weeks. This is the only way to detect operational problems or weaknesses in the program.

9. Use common sense. You don't get something for nothing. Avoid offerings that promise unrealistic returns on your investment. If the profits were so spectacular, the franchisor probably would expand through a personal chain. Nothing can protect you like a large dose of skepticism.

10. Check the track record of other franchisees. How many closed or failed? Did the franchisor "buy back" any franchises? Many franchisors will take back a franchise rather than close it and have a blemish on the record.

Once you have gone through these steps, you will be in a position to assess the risk of losing your $75,000 and the likelihood of earning your $100,000. Remember that it's easy for people to promise. Make them back their promises with hard facts.

9.2   FIVE FRANCHISING DANGER POINTS TO GUARD AGAINST

Q. *I am interested in buying a fast-food franchise from a franchisor with 28 units in operation. I want to know the most likely danger points to watch for.*

A.   Having handled hundreds of franchise deals, I consistently find five trouble spots to anticipate. These are the areas in which you can stumble.

1. *Projected earnings that are inflated:* What the franchisor forecasts as earnings and what you will make may have little in common. Measure those projected earnings against what other franchisees are earning. Franchisors never guarantee profits, but they still use those profits as a sales tool. Your best defense is to get the franchisor to agree to renegotiate the financing terms if you do not reach projected profits.

2. *Capital requirements:* The franchisor will tell you how much capital you'll need to get started. This can be understated by as much as 30 to 40 percent. Carefully review *all* your costs; check them against what other franchisees experienced; and always have a reserve fund available.

3. *Construction delays:* If the franchisor is to construct your unit, insist on a deadline for completion. As with most construction work it usually runs two to three months behind schedule. If the location requires rezoning, you can have even longer delays. What you should demand is that the franchisor pay you your salary during the delay.

4. *Delays in delivery;* This is a common complaint among franchisees. They are contractually obligated to buy from the franchisor, and then the franchisor is late in delivering needed

supplies or inventory. Make certain this isn't a frequent problem in your franchise system and have the contract provide that you can buy "comparable" products from other suppliers if your franchisor cannot make timely delivery.

5. *Inadequate supervision:* You are going into the franchise with the assumption that the franchisor will give you the needed supervision and support services. Frequently, it doesn't happen, particularly if your franchise is geographically isolated from your franchisor's location. With adequate pre-opening training this may not be fatal to your business, but you still are not getting what you paid for. Make certain that your franchise agreement clearly defines what supervision you can expect.

A franchise agreement is a complicated contract and requires experienced legal assistance. Don't be intimidated by the printed form. A reasonable franchisor will change agreements to incorporate the protection you need.

9.3   MUST YOU BUY YOUR PRODUCTS FROM YOUR FRANCHISOR

Q.   *We own a fried chicken franchise. Our franchise agreement specifies that we must purchase certain products from the franchisor. Two of the specific products we must purchase are "take-out" containers and the oil to fry the chicken. We have checked around and find that we can buy comparable products from local suppliers for less money. Are we legally obligated to continue buying from the franchisor?*

A.   The answer to this problem requires a careful look at the items in question. Recent court cases have held that a franchisor can compel a franchisee to use franchisor-supplied products if one of these conditions is met.

1. The product bears the trademark name.

2. The product is of a special formulation, composition, or design that is not precisely duplicated in the products sold on the open market.

The general reasoning is that "special" products used by the franchise system are necessary to retain the uniformity and goodwill of the franchisor's trademark name. The franchisor is also not required to disclose the formulation or content of the special product if it is a trade secret.

Focus on your situation. Is the frying oil or take-out containers of a specific design or formulation, or are they identical to commercial-grade products sold elsewhere? Chances are that the oil has a unique formulation, even if it's only one additional ingredient. The same is probably true of the take-out containers.

If the franchisor demanded that you purchase plain paper bags (without the trademark) or ordinary paper napkins, you could safely switch sources of supply. But first consider the actual cost savings. If the price difference is minimal, it's not worth the challenge; don't overlook the fact that at some point you will want your franchise agreement renewed. So consider the short-term benefits against the long-term consequences.

9.4   HOW MUCH FRANCHISOR CONTROL IS LEGAL

Q. *I own a donut franchise. My problem is that I want to make changes in the operation to increase sales and profits, but the franchisor threatens to terminate my franchise if I do. My ideas are (1) to add hamburgers to the menu to increase lunch sales and (2) to shorten the hours. Can my franchisor stop me?*

A.   The first place to look for the answer is in your franchise agreement. Most franchise agreements either spell out the "dos" and "don'ts" or incorporate the provisions of their operations in a policy manual which provides these guidelines. The courts have routinely held that contractual provisions can legally prevent you from the following.

- Adding or deleting products to be sold
- Changing store hours (except for good cuase)
- Altering franchisor-established prices
- Altering the design or layout of the franchise
- Using equipment not approved by the franchisor
- Using products not approved by the franchisor
- Adhering to a dress code not approved by the franchisor
- Not conforming to reasonable service or promotional policies or programs
- Using a name other than the franchisor's.

In each instance the court has ruled that adherence to reasonable policies established by the franchisor are necessary to preserve the name, goodwill, and reputation of the franchisor's trademark.

If you are dealing with a successful franchise operation, why change it? Many franchisees believe they can make changes that will improve their operations only to find that the franchisor's approach works best. Most franchisors routinely experiment to see what additions to the line or other operational changes can increase profits.

Review your plans with the franchisor and ask what the experiences have been with what you contemplate. The franchisor probably has an answer that makes sense.

9.5   CAN A FRANCHISOR PREVENT YOU FROM SELLING YOUR FRANCHISE

Q. *I have owned a fast-food franchise for several years and, because of a change in career plans, I now want to sell. I have a buyer for the franchise, but the franchisor refuses to approve the buyer. My franchise agreement provides that "the franchi-*

sor must approve any buyer, which approval shall not be un-reasonably withheld." Because the buyer is of excellent credit and character, I believe the failure to approve is unreasonable. The franchisor has offered to buy the franchise back for $10,000 less than I could sell it for. Can I force the sale?

A. You may be in a stronger position than you think. Many courts adopt a lenient attitude on what's "reasonable," knowing that many franchisors are in fact unreasonable so that they force sales back to the franchisors for a low price.

You have a right to demand the reasons why your buyer is not acceptable. If you aren't provided a logical reason, then your only recourse would be to take your franchisor to court. Once you have started suit, your attorney can subpoena the files of other franchisees to determine whether your buyer has the same qualifications as franchisees who are accepted.

A franchisor has the right to refuse transfer to a buyer who does not have the necessary qualifications. Areas that the franchisor can consider are experience, working capital, net worth, business background, education if relevant to operating the franchise, character, and personal background. Of course, a franchisor cannot refuse on the basis of sex, color, race, religion, or national origin.

If the courts find that the franchisor was unreasonable in refusing the transfer to your buyer, or that you were refused in "bad faith," the court can impose additional damages.

CHAPTER
10

Solving

Insurance

Problems

10.1 INSURANCE NEEDS YOU MAY HAVE OVERLOOKED

Q. *Can you summarize the insurance coverage that I should consider, beyond the basic property and liability policies?*

A. Every business must define its own insurance needs, taking into consideration the risk/cost ratio and any special concerns. According to insurance specialists, however, the most commonly overlooked types of insurance include these.

1. *Credit insurance*: This will cover you for bad debts and should be considered to insure the collectibility of an extraordinarily large debt.

2. *Accounts receivable insurance*: This coverage reimburses you for inability to collect receivables due to casualty to your books of account or receivable records.

3. *Profits and commission insurance*: This should be considered if you are a commission agent. It will reimburse you for lost profits in the event that the company you sell for fails to provide the product.

4. *Business interruption insurance*: Will pay your ongoing overhead and lost profits until your business can become operational again following a casualty.

5. *Supplemental perils*: Fire insurance covers only fire. To protect yourself from sprinkler damage or vandalism following a fire, you'll need supplemental perils coverage.

6. *Floater and transit coverage*: This takes several forms. A floater covers goods wherever they are located. A transit policy covers goods only along a specific route.

7. *Bonding insurance*: This is essential to protect yourself from embezzlement by employees having access to large sums of money.

8. *Extended coverage*: Your liability policy will cover you for negligent acts conducted within your place of business. To protect you for wrongful acts beyond your business premises, you may need extended coverage.

You should review your insurance needs annually. As a business grows and takes on new activities and procedures, the insurance needs will also change.

10.2　THE 10 BEST WAYS TO REDUCE INSURANCE COSTS

Q.　*When I purchased my business in 1976, I paid $6,000 a year for casualty insurance. I now pay over $14,000 for the same coverage. Are there any practical ways to reduce my insurance costs?*

A.　You should consider the following cost-cutting techniques.

1. Analyze the cost for each type of insurance you carry. You may find that one form of coverage increased in cost by 300 percent whereas others remained low. You'll then be able to decide what coverage is worthwhile and what should be reduced or eliminated.

2. Increase your deductibles. By absorbing the first $1,000 to $5,000 in losses, you may be able to reduce your premiums substantially.

3. Has your property been reclassified? Fire insurance, for example, is based on the rating for your building. The rating board will consider the neighborhood, tenants, and general condition of the property. Perhaps a bakery opened beside you. This can dramatically increase your rating because of the increased fire hazard. You have a right to check the rating of your property to see whether there are any changes and to contest them.

4. A small investment in sprinklers, fire extinguishers, smoke and fire detectors, or perhaps a fire wall between you

and a high-risk tenant can pay big dividends. Review the possibilities with your insurance company.

5. Take advantage of free programs that can reduce insurance costs. Some companies obtain reduced vehicle insurance premiums by enrolling their drivers in drivers' education classes.

6. If you are located in a "red line" or distressed area, you may be eligible for federal insurance or governmentally subsidized coverage. Inquire at the office of your state insurance commissioner.

7. Do you belong to a trade association? Many companies report substantial savings by joining a "group program" sponsored by their associations. If your association doesn't have such an arrangement, have the association check into it. It can boost membership as well as insurance savings.

8. If you own multiple businesses, you should have a "package policy." This type of coverage can reduce premiums by 25 percent or more.

9. Carry only the insurance you need. As equipment depreciates, you should lower the coverage to conform to those decreasing values. Remember that an insurance company is only obligated to pay the fair value. Any insurance in excess of that fair value is wasted coverage.

10. Shop around. Insurance rates are not fixed (except in a few states). Decide what coverage you want and put it out to bid with five companies. Repeat the process every few years. A company with the lowest rates today may be noncompetitive three years from now.

10.3 WHY ADEQUATE INSURANCE IS ESSENTIAL UNDER A COINSURANCE POLICY

Q. *Our firm owns a building valued at $40,000, and we have insurance on it with the standard 80 percent coinsurance*

*clause. Because of a fire, the building was damaged, and it will
cost us $16,000 to restore it. Because we are insured for
$24,000, I expect the insurance company to pay the full
$16,000 to restore the building, but they claim they are on-
ly liable for $12,000. Wouldn't they be liable for the full
$16,000?*

A.   No. By my calculations the insurance company is correct
in offering only $12,000. When you agreed to the 80 percent
coinsurance clause, you agreed to insure the building for 80
percent of its value, or $32,000. Because you only carried $24,-
000 in insurance, you have only three-quarters of the required
insurance. Therefore, the insurance company has the right to
pay you only the same three-quarters of the loss, or $12,000.

Business people carrying 80 percent coinsurance policies
should have their properties appraised annually and make
certain that the insurance coverage is raised to 80 percent
of that new valuation. Then they have the protection they
bargained for.

10.4   HOW TO START A SELF-INSURANCE PROGRAM

Q.   *Our firm is considering dropping all insurance coverage
(except mandatory motor vehicle insurance) and self-insuring
instead. What experiences have other companies had with self-
insurance?*

A.   Recent management studies show that with skyrocketing
insurance costs more and more firms are using the self-insure
option. Before you decide on self-insurance, carefully assess
your present coverage and the potential for loss under each
plan. Your strategy should be to self-insure for losses that are
not likely and for those that you can absorb.

Many companies limit their self-insurance exposure to four
to five percent of their net working capital. Others use one-half

to one percent pretax profits. You will have to define your own limits of acceptable loss.

Almost all self-insurance companies establish a reserve fund. Instead of paying the insurance company, they pay the "premiums" into the reserve fund with the expectation that losses will not exceed 50 percent of the reserve. Because you will be paying the funds into the reserve fund, you won't alleviate cash flow.

Insurance is a tax-deductible expense, but payments into your reserve fund will not be deductible. Any loss or casualty suffered, however, will be deductible when you self-insure.

Insolvent companies should always self-insure, unless they are required to carry insurance under the terms of their loan agreements. There's no logic in insuring a business worth $100,000 when debts exceed the $100,000. All you are doing is using needed dollars to buy insurance to protect your creditors' interests.

Before you self-insure, check your lease and loan agreements, as they may require insurance coverage and you will need the appropriate waivers to avoid a default. The decision to self-insure should also be voted by the board of directors, and it's wise to obtain even stockholder approval to avoid a charge of mismanagement if an extensive loss should occur.

10.5 WHEN YOUR INSURANCE COMPANY MAY BE LIABLE FOR MORE THAN THE POLICY COVERAGE

Q. *Our firm carries vehicle collision insurance in the amount of $100,000. Because of the negligent driving of one of our employees, the company was sued for $300,000. The plaintiff recovered a judgment for $180,000, so we had to pay the excess $80,000 over the policy limits. We now found that, prior to trial, the plaintiff offered to settle for $75,000, and our insur-*

ance company never even notified us of the settlement offer. Do we have recourse against our insurance company?

A. You may. Most cases hold that an insurance company can be liable to its insured under either of the following.

1. If it fails to communicate offers of settlement, even though the insurance company would be paying the settlement.

2. If it acts either negligently or in "bad faith" (depending on jurisdiction) in settling a claim.

Whether the insurance company acted either negligently or in bad faith in refusing to settle for $75,000 would depend on a realistic assessment of the case when the offer was made. If reasonably prudent attorneys or insurance adjusters would agree that the case most likely would bring a recovery in excess of $75,000, the mere fact that your insurance company guessed wrong is not sufficient to make a claim.

This case points out the importance of an insured party's having total familiarity with the progress of a case against the insured, particularly if the insured may not have enough insurance to cover the claim. Always ask your insurance company to provide you with pleadings and correspondence and have these reviewed by your own counsel. Your attorney may be able to convince the insurance company to settle within the policy limits and avoid you liability in excess of the policy limits.

10.6 WHEN TO USE KEY EMPLOYEE INSURANCE

Q. *Our mail order firm has a marketing director who is amongst the best in her field. We are not concerned about her leaving the company, but we do want protection in the event of her death. How can we obtain that protection?*

A. Key employee insurance is what you need. The theory behind this type of insurance is that the insured is an asset to the company and has a definable value. Generally, the company pays the premium and names itself beneficiary.

The policy should be for an amount approximating the value of the employee to the company, as you may not have an insurable interest if the amount is clearly excessive. Insurance premiums are deductible to the company, but proceeds of the policy may be taxed as income.

CHAPTER

11

Tax Tactics That Can Work For You

11.1 HOW THE NEW TAX LAWS ALLOW YOU TO TAKE FASTER WRITE-OFFS ON BUSINESS ASSETS

Q. *What depreciation schedule can we take on the various business assets our corporation owns? We understand the new tax laws have accelerated the depreciation periods.*

A. Under the new tax laws you can take the fastest "write-offs" possible under the Accelerated Cost Recovery System. Business vehicles can be depreciated over a three-year period (25 percent during the fist year, 38 percent the second, and 37 percent the third). Equipment, fixtures, and furniture can be depreciated over a five-year period. Buildings can now be depreciated over 15 years.

You have the option to spread the depreciation over a longer time period if you prefer, but then you'll be paying more taxes than necessary during the early years in exchange for profit protection in later years. In addition to the depreciation you can take an investment credit on new equipment for years that the investment credit is in effect.

You have another alternative. You can "expense" up to $5,000 in depreciable assets in the first year instead of writing it off over a number of years. For example, if you purchase a $5,000 word processor, you can elect to expense the entire $5,000 in the first year instead of depreciating it over five. When you expense the item rather than depreciating it, however, you do lose the investment credit.

The $5,000 write-off extends through 1983, increases to $7,500 in 1984 and 1985, and climbs to $10,000 in 1986 and thereafter.

11.2 HOW TO USE YEAR-END DEFERRALS TO SAVE TAXES

Q. *We operate our small manufacturing plant on a "cash basis" rather than on "accrual." What year-end strategies can help us reduce taxes for the current year?*

A. One possible strategy would be to pay all your bills before the end of the year and defer income by discouraging collection of receivables until the beginning of the next accounting cycle. If you file on the accrual method, you can essentially accomplish the same result by deferring contracts or completed work.

The obvious problem with accelerating payments while deferring income is that you may end up with a cash flow problem while you are trying to save on taxes. Further, relaxation of collection efforts on receivables may create bad debts that would otherwise have been collectible through aggressive collection efforts. Business owners also point to the high cost of interest as another argument against deferring receivables.

Although it's true that constant deferral of year-end taxes can cause cash flow problems, you may have the advantage of pushing your tax bill into a year with lower taxable profits. Further, the longer you have use of the tax savings, the longer you have an interest-free loan from Uncle Sam.

11.3 HOW DOES A SUB-CHAPTER S CORPORATION WORK?

Q. *Our accountant has recommended that we set our business up as a "Sub-Chapter S" corporation. What are its benefits, and how does it work?*

A. If a corporation elects to be taxed as a Sub-Chapter S, the corporation will enjoy the benefits of avoiding income tax liability on its profits. Essentially, the corporation is treated as a sole proprietorship (if one stockholder) or a partnership (if multiple stockholders). Profits and losses of the corporation are passed directly to the stockholders, who must take the corporate profits as reportable income whether they received the profits or not. Corporate losses are treated as an ordinary business loss to the owners, to the extent of their investment.

Sub-Chapter S is not for everyone. It's usually used when the business is expected to lose money during its start-up years. The owners can deduct these losses from personal income. Once the business becomes profitable, the corporation may drop the Sub-Chapter S so that the owners won't have personal tax liability on the profits the business generates. At that point, however, the corporation will have its own liability for income taxes.

Since Sub-Chapter S is only an IRS provision, you operate your company like any other corporation, and of course you still have the protection of limited liability. It's only in the area of taxation that Sub-Chapter S makes a difference.

Not every corporation qualifies for Sub-Chapter S treatment. Here are the basic requirements.

1. Initially the corporation must have 10 or fewer stockholders; the number can be increased to 15 after five years. Therefore, no publicly held corporation will qualify.

2. The shares must be owned by individuals, estates, or certain types of trusts.

3. The corporation must be domestic and not part of an affiliated group eligible to file a consolidated tax return.

4. The corporation must have only one class of stock.

5. At least 20 percent of its income must come from sources within the U.S.

6. The corporation cannot be engaged primarily in real estate.

Before your accountant decides on a Sub-Chapter S, make certain he or she is fully familiar with your own personal tax situation and can show you how the Sub-Chapter S election will save you tax dollars.

11.4 SHOULD YOU USE THE CORPORATE CAR AS YOUR FAMILY CAR

Q. *Do you recommend having the corporation buy a new car if we plan to use it approximately 50 percent of the time for personal and family use?*

A. Many tax advisors now recommend against corporate ownership of a car that will be used more than nominally for personal use. Increasingly, the IRS is challenging the corporate deduction for the vehicle, even when the corporation is reimbursed for the personal use on a mileage basis.

There are also insurance considerations. In some instances the IRS has disallowed settlement payments as an expense when the corporate car was involved in an accident during personal use. Finally, the corporate stockholders may question the use of a corporate vehicle for personal use, even though the corporation is being reimbursed.

Corporate ownership of the vehicle may be indicated when it will be used at least 70 to 80 percent of the time for business purposes, when you also have a family-owned car, and when you faithfully reimburse the corporation for the personal use. If you decide to own the car personally, the corporation can reimburse you for mileage costs, and this undoubtedly will raise fewer questions.

11.5 WHEN YOU CAN DEDUCT EMPLOYEE MEALS CONSUMED ON THE BUSINESS PREMISES

Q. *Many of our clerical employees are provided meals to be eaten at their desks, as cyclical peak workloads prevent them*

*from taking their conventional lunch hours. It's my under-
standing that we can deduct the cost of the meals we provide.
Is this correct?*

A. You are entitled to deduct your cost for meals you furnish
employees if it's "necessary" or "convenient" to have them on
the premises during their lunch hour. If there is no need to
have the employees present or if they have full opportunity to
leave the premises to purchase their own meals, the value of
the meals must be treated as income to the employees and is
subject to income, Social Security, and unemployment taxes.

11.6   HOW TO LEND TO YOUR OWN CORPORATION

Q. *I will have to advance my corporation over $100,000 to
handle its cash flow problems over the next two years. How
should these loans be set up to protect me from an IRS challenge and to give me maximum legal protection?*

A. For the tax angle you want the loan to stand as a "bona
fide" lender–borrower transaction. This will give you the right
to repay yourself without taxable consequence, except for the
interest payments, which will be taxable income to you and an
interest expense for the corporation. Here are some guidelines
to follow.

1. Don't let your total loans exceed 90 percent of all funds
you put into the business, inclusive of capital for the shares.
A safer rule to follow is a maximum debt-to-equity ratio of
70 to 30.

2. Document the transaction by taking a promissory note
from the corporation. Have all the documentation you would
demand in any other "arms-length" transaction.

3. Have the note bear interest somewhere between 12 and
22 percent. It doesn't have to be as high as a bank would

charge, but it's difficult to justify a loan at less than 12 percent. You can "tie" the rate to a floating prime rate if you prefer.

4. The note should run between 6 and 15 years. You'll have no problem with long-term notes, but the IRS may challenge you once you shorten the note to less than 5 years.

5. Make certain your accountant reflects the loan on the financial statement and tax returns.

6. You can increase the protection for your loan by securing it with a security interest (mortgage) on business assets. This will give you first claim on the asset proceeds should the business fail.

According to the IRS most "loans" are disqualified and treated as dividend income because the owners did not "lend" the money on a commercially reasonable basis, lacked loan documentation, or charged little or no interest for the loan.

11.7 WHEN SALARIES ARE TREATED AS TAXABLE PROFITS

Q. *As owner of a corporation manufacturing drapery materials, I draw a salary of $50,000. The corporation only shows a nominal profit. Can the IRS declare part of my salary as profits taxable to the corporation?*

A. They can try. You have a right to a "reasonable" salary, but beyond that excessive salaries become just another way of shielding corporate profits from taxation and can be contested.

What is a reasonable salary? The IRS will consider several factors.

- What skill, education, or experience is required
- What it would cost to replace you with a person of equal skill and managerial competence
- The size of the company
- The profits your company did declare

- Whether your salary decision was controlled by you or an "arms-length" board of directors
- Comparable salaries paid to other CEOs in similar companies of equal size.

Generally the IRS won't challenge the salary if it's slightly on the high side, but once it becomes obviously excessive, it can easily "trigger" a corporate tax audit.

You may also be tempted to draw money out of the corporation by having members of the family on the payroll. For example, if you need $15,000 annually to send your 18-year-old son to college, it would take $30,000 in salary (assuming you're in the 50 percent tax bracket) to generate that $15,000. You may decide your son should go on the payroll, and he could draw out his $15,000 with little tax consequence. Under an audit the IRS will take a hard look to make certain your son actually worked and that $15,000 represents fair salary for that work.

11.8   YOUR PERSONAL LIABILITY FOR CORPORATE TAXES

Q. A year ago my printing plant was liquidated in bankruptcy, and at that time it owed the IRS about $20,000 in withholding taxes and the state approximately $12,000 in withholding and sales tax. The IRS and the state are now demanding that I personally pay these taxes. I thought a corporation insulated me from corporate obligations.

A. You're correct, but there are some important exceptions. Two obvious exceptions are obligations you personally guarantee and claims arising from your own personal wrongdoing (for example, negligence, deceit, or larceny).

Taxes are the third big exception. An officer of the corporation (the president or treasurer) is personally liable for any unpaid "trust" taxes owed either the IRS or the state. Trust taxes are those collected from others to be turned over to the taxing authorities. These include

- Withholding taxes and employees' contributions to FICA (Social Security and unemployment)
- Sales and use tax
- State unemployment taxes.

You generally are not liable for taxes that are the direct tax obligation of the corporation. These include

- Income taxes
- Corporate excise or franchise taxes
- The corporation's contributions to FICA or Social Security.

You may find that on the tax due the IRS, 20 to 25 percent of that $20,000 is the corporation's contribution to FICA, and you have no personal obligation on that. Make certain to point that out to the IRS.

If a taxing authority is unable to collect from the corporation, it will convert the tax liability to a 100 percent personal assessment and can proceed against you in the same manner as unpaid personal income taxes. Theoretically, the IRS can prosecute criminally for unpaid trust taxes, but it very rarely does. What collection rights and practices your state may use should be reviewed by your attorney, as this will require reference to state law. Here's the approach you or your attorney should take.

1. Check with the bankruptcy trustee to see whether there are sufficient proceeds in the estate to pay the taxes (taxes have a priority after payment of secured debts, expenses of administration and fees, and wages owed).

2. If there are proceeds that will be available for the taxing authorities, make certain the IRS and state file a "proof of claim" with the trustee so that they can be paid.

3. If the proceeds from the bankruptcy court will not be sufficient to pay the taxes, then have your accountant determine what portion of the tax bill is represented by trust

taxes. That's the amount for which you will be personally liable.

4. Communicate with the taxing authorities. With a cooperative spirit you may be able to work out a favorable "long-term" payout.

From my experiences, I have noted that the majority of small businesses do have outstanding tax liabilities once the business fails. Personal liability can be avoided by adhering to these guidelines.

1. Pay the taxes when due. Deposit the tax in an account on a weekly basis so that you won't be tempted to use tax funds for your own cash flow purposes.

2. Don't remain an officer of a corporation that's falling behind on its taxes, unless, of course, it's your own corporation and you have no choice.

3. Don't sign checks as a bookkeeper or comptroller, as the IRS can personally assess even a bookkeeper who is not an officer if it concludes the bookkeeper had complete check-writing authority.

A final point: Unlike income taxes that are dischargeable in bankruptcy if more than three years old, you cannot discharge through bankruptcy your personal tax liability for corporate taxes.

11.9 HOW SECTION 1244 STOCK CAN HELP YOU

Q. *My lawyer recently had me sign a statement acknowledging that the shares of stock issued to me from my corporation were issued pursuant to Section 1244 of the Internal Revenue Code. What does this mean?*

A. This type of stock will give you maximum tax protection if your business fails. With Section 1244 stock you can deduct the total loss of your investment as an ordinary business loss to be fully offset against taxable income in the year you experienced the loss.

For example, let's suppose you invested $50,000 for your shares. Should your business fail, you can deduct the $50,000 from income. If you don't acquire your shares under Section 1244, you can only deduct up to $3,000 a year in losses against ordinary income. At that rate it would take you about 17 years to "write-off" your loss.

There are absolutely no disadvantages to Section 1244 shares, and every business person should be certain of having that protection when incorporating.

11.10　HOW LEASING EQUIPMENT TO YOUR OWN CORPORATION CAN PROVIDE YOU A TAX SHELTER

Q. *I operate a printing plant that requires a $60,000 press. I am undecided as to whether to have the corporation own it or to buy it personally and lease it to the corporation. Which method do you suggest?*

A. To answer that question requires knowing your tax bracket and that of your corporation. Chances are, however, that you have the higher tax bracket, as small corporations only pay a 15 to 16 percent tax on profits.

If you purchase the equipment personally (or through a special trust that your lawyer can easily set up), you can deduct the 10 percent investment credit and use both an accelerated depreciation and the interest on any loan required to finance the purchase (see question 11.1). Against this you will have to report the income that the corporation will pay you for rent. Structured properly, the expenses should greatly exceed the income, giving you a healthy "paper" loss that can be an effective tax shelter on your personal taxes.

Once the equipment is fully depreciated, you can sell the equipment to the corporation for a nominal price, and the income generated from the sale will be taxed at a low capital gains rate.

That's the purpose of leasing to your own corporation. Equipment can provide substantial paper losses, and in most cases those losses can be better applied against your personal income than against your corporate income. To avoid a challenge by the IRS, make certain your accountant approves the terms of the lease, as you are dealing with a technical tax matter.

11.11 WHY EMPLOYEE BENEFITS ARE WORTH MORE THAN RAISES

Q. Do you recommend fringe benefits be increased instead of giving employees raises and allowing them to buy their own insurance?

A. It's usually better for both employer and employee if the employer provides benefits that qualify as an expense deduction. Your employees don't have to pay taxes on the value of the benefits, and you save the cost of Social Security and unemployment contributions that you otherwise would have had to pay on those salary increases.

Group medical and life insurance are common fringe benefits, but you may want to consider these often overlooked fringe benefit possibilities.

1. *Group legal plans:* A qualified legal plan will give you and your employees coverage for personal legal services.

2. *Dues and subscriptions:* Paying for memberships and magazines relating to the employee's job or the business of the employer is an allowed expense item, and it's seldom questioned upon audit.

3. *Educational expenses:* You can now deduct expenses for courses that your employees take if the courses are job related. It's now also possible to take a "write-off" on educational courses that are not job related as long as the employee owns five percent or less of the stock of the corporation.

4. *Discounts:* Consider offering your employees discounts on merchandise you sell. This can be a valuable, tax-free fringe benefit to employees working in the retail trade.

Your objective should be gradually to add these or other valuable fringe benefits instead of granting salary increases. At least such fringes can reduce the amount of the raises.

11.12 HOW TO STOP THE TAX COLLECTOR

Q. *We owe the IRS over $27,000 for back withholding taxes. Every few weeks the IRS levies our checking account, and now the IRS is threatening to seize and auction the business to collect the back taxes. What can we do to stop this?*

A. Consider these possibilities.

1. You may be able to stop the levies by withdrawing your funds from the checking account and opening a new account in a bank that is not close to you. All future payments to the IRS should be through money orders that cannot be traced to your new bank. The IRS keeps a record of what banks your tax checks are drawn on so that it can identify the bank on which to serve the levy. If the IRS doesn't know where you keep your funds, it will be more difficult to serve a levy. There is nothing illegal in keeping your banking relationships confidential, and I have seen this same technique work many times.

2. For taxes not paid within 10 days of demand, the IRS does have the power to seize. But even the IRS looks at that as a last resort if all else fails.

Most revenue agents will accept a payout as long as it's reasonable and you stay current on future tax obligations. The one instance in which the IRS is quick to seize is a situation in which you continue to fall further behind in your tax payments. Few people can call that unreasonable.

Have your accountant prepare a cash flow statement to support the reasonableness of your installment payback. The IRS may give you two to three years if you are believed to be negotiating in good faith. Make this a condition of your agreement that all future taxes will be deposited weekly into a bank account.

If your agent refuses the proposition, go to the agent's superior. You have nothing to lose at that point, and you will often obtain satisfaction higher in the bureaucracy.

If your business is financed by the Small Business Administration (SBA), this may help. The IRS will often cooperate more with an SBA-financed business on the theory that collecting the taxes may simply be causing a loss for another federal agency through a forced liquidation of the business.

Should all else fail, you can file for protection under Chapter 11 of the Bankruptcy Code. This will automatically stop all collection efforts by the IRS, but you will be obligated to stay current on taxes under the protection of the bankruptcy court.

The IRS can be intimidating, and the laws do back any IRS threats. Your best defense is logic and demonstrating both a willingness and an ability to pay the taxes. All the IRS wants is money. Your job is to show that the money can just as easily come from operating the business as from liquidating it.

Remember that, as a corporate officer, you are personally liable for withholding taxes (see question 11.8). So if you do anticipate a business failure, you should give priority to paying the back taxes, not to establishing better cash flow before the business fails.

CHAPTER
12

Your
Checking Account
and the Law

12.1 TWELVE WAYS TO AVOID BAD CHECKS

Q. *Can you recommend a policy to cut down on the number of "bad" checks we accept?*

A. Some leading banks and security specialists recommend this policy.

1. Don't accept out-of-state checks.

2. Limit the check to the amount of the purchase unless you provide a check-cashing service.

3. Don't accept temporary checks or what is obviously a check from a new account (low-numbered checks and checks without a depositor's imprint are certain clues).

4. Don't accept second-party checks (a check made out to your customer to be endorsed over to you).

5. Positive identification is essential. A driver's license can prove identity through its picture, driver's license number, or Social Security number. Back it up with another form of identification; a credit card is best, for it shows credit worthiness.

6. Record the necessary information on the check.
   - Local address
   - Telephone number
   - Social Security or driver's license number
   - Credit card and number

7. Delegate check cashing to one person. This person should have the training and responsibility to approve all checks.

8. Limit checks to a maximum amount. Don't gamble more than you can afford to lose.

9. Use common sense. Dress, demeanor, and the nature of the purchase are all clues as to the likelihood of the check's being good.

10. Subscribe to a check credit service. With a phone call you can find whether the customer has a history of passing bad checks. Your bank can give you the names of companies offering this service in your area; the cost is nominal.

11. Consider check insurance. Some insurance companies will "insure" against bad checks, and the cost is low.

12. Follow up. Turn to question 12.2 to find the recommended procedures once you have a bad check to deal with.

12.2 THE RIGHT WAY TO HANDLE BAD CHECKS

Q. *As a distributor of flowers and plants to retailers, we often run into a "bad check" problem. Some accounts do have charge privileges with us, and when they pay on their accounts their checks sometimes bounce. We also have accounts that buy on a COD basis and pay us with bad checks. What is the best way to collect on bad checks?*

A. There are several things you can do effectively to collect on bad checks. Of course, your first step is to reduce the number of bad checks you get. In question 12.1 I show you just how to accomplish that. Once a check is returned, however, you should follow these steps.

1. Determine why the check was returned. If it's marked "uncollected funds," this simply means that the depositor had ample funds on deposit but that the funds were represented by other checks that have not yet cleared. "Insufficient funds" means that the depositor does not have enough funds to cover the check. "Account closed" means that the check you're holding is absolutely worthless.

2. If the check is marked "insufficient" or "uncollected," which is the usual case, then my advice is *not* to redeposit it. The reason for this is that, if you do redeposit it and the account is still without good funds, it will only come back to you once again unpaid, and banks won't let you deposit a check more than twice. You are therefore left with the alternative of replacing the check.

3. A better strategy is not to put the check in for collection unless you are certain it will be honored. You can do this yourself by calling the issuer's bank on a daily basis and asking whether the check is "good." Once you hear that good funds are available, I recommend you immediately go to the bank and present it for payment. If you deposit the check, it will take two to three days to reach the bank, and by then there may again be insufficient funds. If this is too laborious a process for you, then give the check to your bank and say that you want to "place it for collection." They will then call the issuer's bank each day for up to 10 days. Once your bank ascertains the check is good, the bank will deposit it for you.

Assuming the check is still unpaid after 10 days, I'd say that stronger collection methods are in order.

1. If the check was for a COD purchase, you will certainly have a criminal remedy. Here you will have to consult local law, as most states require you to give the issuer written notice before you institute criminal process. Once notified of the bad check, some people will try to make a deal whereby they will pay the check "off" in installments. For you this can be a mistake. Once you accept a partial payment on a bad check, many courts will say that you have elected a civil remedy and cannot now use a criminal process. If your account wants to pay it off in installments, it's best to give the account an extended period to accumulate the entire amount. If this works, then that's the end of the problem. If your account defaults, you still have your criminal remedies.

2. If the check is for a past debt, you probably can only sue civilly, as most states do not consider it criminal unless you

simultaneously parted with something of value in exchange for the check. If it's a small enough amount, you should go through small claims court; otherwise you'll have to forward it to your attorney to commence suit.

3. Maintain your inquiry at the issuer's bank. I have seen many situations in which a check wasn't good for as long as two to three months. Suddenly, the issuer makes an unusually large deposit, and the check is then good. Take a tip from the IRS. They like to put liens on checking accounts on Mondays. The reason is obvious. For most businesses this represents the day of their biggest deposits, after weekend receipts!

Here are some other do's and don'ts to follow:

1. Don't mark a bill or statement "paid" if it's paid by check. The correct procedure is to stamp it "paid by check." This makes it conditional.

2. Don't communicate your problems with a bad check passer to a third party. This can expose you to a slander action.

3. Don't try to reclaim the goods you sold on the strength of the bad check. Unfortunately, the buyer has good title even though he or she didn't pay. I once had a client who sold over $12,000 worth of computer equipment on a COD basis and received for it a bad check. When the check bounced, he showed up with two men and forcibly removed the computer. He ended up with a criminal record on a larceny charge.

4. Do act fast and decisively. In many instances, whether the check ultimately will be made good will depend upon the issuer's perception about how far you will go to collect. If you have a criminal remedy, let the issuer know that you'll use it.

12.3   SIX INSTANCES IN WHICH YOUR BANK IS LIABLE IF IT DOES PAY YOUR CHECK

Q. *Under what circumstances would my bank have to reimburse my account if it wrongfully honors one of my checks?*

I gave a supplier a postdated check for $800. The bank cashed the check before the due date, but I intended to place a "stop payment" on the check, as the supplier did not deliver the promised goods.

A. Most courts would hold your bank liable for honoring a check before the due date, as the bank is only authorized to cash the check upon presentment on or after the due date. Until then you had the right to put a stop payment on the check. Your bank also will be obligated to repay you under the following circumstances.

1. *Forged signature:* No matter how authentic the signature may be, if it is not yours, the bank is liable. If you allowed the forgery to come about through your own negligence, that can be a defense. To impose liability on the bank, you must also notify the bank within a reasonable time of discovery.

2. *Payment on a missing endorsement:* A bank is liable when it pays a check missing a required endorsement.

3. *Payment after a stop payment:* Once you have a valid stop payment on a check, the bank is liable if it thereafter pays the check. A spoken stop order is only good for 14 days, and a written order is effective only for six months and should be renewed thereafter. The burden is on you to prove you made a timely stop payment.

4. *Alteration:* If you make out a check for $500 and the payee alters it to read $5,000, the bank would be liable for the excess $4,500. The defenses of your negligence or failure to give timely notice to the bank can be a defense, as with forgery.

5. *Death of the depositor:* A bank cannot pay a check after the depositor dies and the bank has reasonable notice of that fact. Where the depositor is a corporation, the death of the signatory will not apply.

Considering your rights against the bank for wrongfully paying on a check, you should examine each check after it has been paid to make certain that it is properly paid. Should you find a check that should not have been paid, give the bank immediate written notice; otherwise you may lose your rights.

12.4   YOUR RIGHTS WHEN A CHECK IS NOT PAID

Q.   We recently cashed a $600 payroll check drawn on a corporate account. The employee properly endorsed the check over to us when we cashed it, but the company that issued the check has a "stop payment" against it. What's our next step?

A.   You have rights against both the company and the employee as endorser. Very few defenses the company can raise would be good against you. For example, if the company claimed a breach of contract by the employee, that would be a good defense for not paying the employee, but you would have better rights to collect.

The employee, upon endorsing the check, warranted that if the company doesn't pay the check, he or she will. That's one reason for obtaining the endorsement. You should give the employee timely notice that the check wasn't paid and demand that it be paid. If the employee refuses, you should file a small claims action against both the company and the employee. You'll certainly recover judgment against the employee and most likely against the company that issued the check.

To protect your rights to collect on a check, follow these guidelines.

1. Always obtain endorsement of the party negotiating the check to you.

2. Make demand on the "drawer" of the check for payment (see question 12.2).

3. Give immediate notice that the check has been dishonored to all endorsers and include a demand for payment.

4. Don't give up your claim because the drawer of the check gives you a reason for nonpayment. If you gave good value for the check and accepted it without knowledge of any problem, only certain defenses, such as forgery or alteration, will be good against you.

12.5 CAN YOU SAFELY IGNORE A RELEASE ENDORSEMENT ON A CHECK

Q. *We have an account that owes us $4,000, although she has contested her bill. She finally sent us a check for $2,500 and on the reverse side marked "in full payment and discharge of all debts due." We don't know whether simply to strike out the "release" language or to ingore it. What do you recommend?*

A. I recommend neither approach unless you are willing to settle for $2,500. You have no right to alter a check. You either have to accept it as is or send it back.

It's equally dangerous to deposit the check with that clause. Technically, release language will not operate as a release if the debt is undisputed and unliquidated. Most courts have abandoned that theory and hold that, if you accept a check subject to conditions, you are bound by those conditions.

To be on the safe side, your account should have indicated on the check that it was "full settlement of a disputed claim." Then acceptance of a lower amount would discharge the entire debt.

12.6 YOU MAY HAVE A SPECIAL LIABILITY WHEN ACCEPTING GOVERNMENT CHECKS

Q. *Our supermarket cashed a U.S. government Social Security check that was endorsed to us by a customer. The Treasury Department, claiming the check was stolen and forged, now wants us to repay to them the amount of the check. Are we liable for the repayment?*

A. Yes. A party presenting a government check for payment guarantees to the government that all prior endorsements on the check are genuine. If it turns out that any endorsements are forged, even if it's through the government's own negligence, the government can demand payment.

For this reason you should take special cautions in accepting a government check. Make certain through proper identification that the person endorsing the check is the named payee and never accept a check with a prior endorsement, as you have no way of knowing whether it's genuine.

12.7 HOW TO ENDORSE A CHECK WHEN YOUR NAME IS STATED INCORRECTLY

Q. *Because most of our invoices are paid by check, we find that customers frequently make out their checks incorrectly. Instead of properly labeling the check to H. Smith Co., Inc., we receive checks made out to "Smith & Company," "Smith Corporation," and every other possible combination. Can we endorse a check that doesn't properly state our name?*

A. Providing the issuer of the check intended the check to be payable to you, you can endorse the check. The proper procedure is to endorse the check with the incorrect name with parenthesis around it and then endorse the check again with your correct corporate name.

12.8   WHEN A BANK CAN STOP PAYMENT ON A CERTIFIED CHECK

Q.   *We sold $6,000 in merchandise on a COD basis and required the buyer to give us a certified check. When we attempted to cash the check, the bank refused to pay on it and claimed that the depositor asked the bank not to honor it because the goods we sold were allegedly defective. Can the bank refuse to pay a check if certified?*

A.   Not under these circumstances. A bank issuing a certified check cannot raise the defenses that would be available to the customer. The only reason for which a bank can refuse to pay a properly endorsed and presented certified check is that the bank suspects the amount of the check has been altered.

Some banks will ignore their liability and refuse to pay on a certified check at the insistence of a customer, as long as the customer adequately indemnifies the bank for any liability it may incur through its wrongful refusal to pay. From my experiences a letter to the banking commission should get you fast results.

CHAPTER
13

Collecting

What's Owed You

13.1 DON'T ASK THE WRONG QUESTIONS WHEN EXTENDING CREDIT

Q. *Because of increased competition our retail appliance store will soon offer charge privileges. Are there any restrictions on determining who is credit worthy?*

A. Fortunately, you weigh all the factors and make the final decision. The federal Equal Credit Opportunity Act does, however, prevent you from

- Disregarding income from an applicant's part-time employment
- Denying credit on the basis of sex, marital status, age, religion, or race
- Denying credit on the basis of a spouse's credit history. (In fact it's illegal to inquire about the spouse's credit history or financial condition unless the spouse will be obligated on the debt. You should always maintain separate credit files for spouses.)

Most states have enacted laws that prevent discrimination against borrowers who are on welfare programs.

An added caution: As part of your credit procedure you must inform the applicant that you may seek an investigative report, what an investigative or credit report consists of, and that the applicant has the right to an "accurate and complete" disclosure describing the nature of the investigation. Should the applicant request that disclosure, you have five days to respond.

13.2 SELF-PROTECTION WHEN GRANTING CREDIT

Q. *Uncollectible receivables are up 20 percent over last year in our wholesale novelty business. What steps can we take to reduce bad debts?*

A. An effective credit and collection policy is required even in a good economy but becomes considerably more important when money is tight. Credit managers and attorneys suggest these loss-reducing techniques.

1. *Check credit:* Forget customer references, for even an insolvent account can find several references. I recommend TRW and Dun & Bradstreet as commercial rating services. Even established accounts should have an updated check, as credit ratings do change.

2. *Obtain direct credit information:* Develop your own credit application. It can give you valuable information that creditor services may not be able to provide, and if the account falsifies the information, you have strong criminal and civil remedies.

3. *Try for partial prepayments:* Many firms now require 25 to 50 percent of the order to be prepaid. This not only weeds out the more obvious "credit risks," but it also accelerates cash flow.

4. *Cut orders:* This is another increasingly common technique. Smaller orders and more frequent deliveries will reduce your exposure, particularly if you go on "order to order" terms.

5. *Bargain for security:* Extensive credit requires security. Bargain for a security interest on assets or for a guarantee from the principals. A security interest with adequate collateral behind it is your best protection.

6. *Accelerate billing:* Instead of once-a-month billing, consider billing on a biweekly basis. Invoices with shipments may also decrease bad debts through accelerated payments.

7. *Watch your credit limits:* Every customer must have a defined credit limit, and this must be carefully maintained.

8. *Increase cash discounts:* The standard is 2 percent for 10-day payments, but many firms are reporting excellent results with 5 percent for cash. If you do offer a larger cash discount, it must be offered to all your accounts.

9. *Settle questionable accounts:* Once an account gets into financial trouble, try to liquidate the debt quickly for as much as possible, even if you have to do it with a 20 to 30 percent discount. The 70 cents on the dollar you may get today may evaporate into nothing tomorrow.

10. *Remember the "squeaky wheel" theory:* Once an account falls behind, persist with a "get tough" collection policy to get your money. In a financial crisis your accounts will pay the aggressive creditors first and let the others wait. You have to decide whether you want that aggressive approach or would prefer to wait and just watch your bad debts continue to mount.

13.3   WHEN YOU SHOULD AND SHOULD NOT USE COLLECTION AGENCIES

Q. *Our lumber company has over 3,000 charge customers ranging from building contractors to home owners. We experience about a 5 percent bad debt loss. Do you recommend a collection agency to collect overdue accounts?*

A.   My answer may not make me popular with the collection agency industry, but you probably will do better by finding an aggressive collection lawyer who's willing to take all your accounts.

The reason I discourage collection agencies is that they only serve the function of "middle person" in the collection process, and for their involvement you will have to pay 25 to 40 percent of whatever they collect. The problem is that, if they are unsuccessful in collecting, they will have to forward the claims to an attorney who will then charge you another 25 to 33 percent. Before you're through, your stake in the claim is down to 40 to 50 percent. My experiences show that the best collection procedure is this.

1. Try "in-house" collection efforts first. Design two or three "tough" collection letters to send out.

2. Follow with a phone call to see whether you can arrange a payment plan. If you do reach a payout agreement, send the account a letter confirming the terms. This not only creates a "psychological commitment" but could be used in court to show that an agreement was reached and that obviously the account has no defense to your claim.

3. For accounts with which you are unsuccessful, direct referral to an attorney will be required. If your corporate lawyer does not specialize in collections, your lawyer can find an aggressive firm that does specialize in your type of collection. Negotiate a "package" arrangement with the attorney. I have found the best arrangement to be this.

- Offer a 15 percent commission on all monies received if only a letter is required.
- If suit becomes necessary, expect the fee to be about 25 percent. This is the recommended rate of the Commercial Law League, a national association of collection lawyers.
- Don't expect the attorney to go to court on claims under $200 to $300, as it just isn't cost justified. If there are many accounts that can be processed in small claims court on the same day, then it may be worth the time, but leave that to your attorney's judgment.
- You will have to pay all court costs, filing fees, and process servers' fees whether you collect or not.

The two instances in which collection agencies can be worth the expense are these.

- Small accounts that no attorney will bother with.
- Out-of-state accounts for which you don't have an attorney in that state to handle the matter.

13.4 SHOULD YOU EXTEND CREDIT TO A COMPANY BEING REORGANIZED UNDER CHAPTER 11

Q. *We have a retail account that owes us $65,000 in past bills and filed for reorganization under Chapter 11 of the Bankruptcy Code. The account now wants us to sell additional goods on credit and claims that we are fully protected. Are they correct?*

A. Not necessarily. Debts incurred after filing of a Chapter 11 do have a "priority" status and are not subject to the debt-reducing treatment of debts incurred prior to the filing. Notwithstanding the priority status of subsequently incurred debts, that does not guarantee payment in the event the company fails and goes into a "straight" bankruptcy.

Before subsequently incurred debts can be paid, other preferred claimants have to be paid. These include holders of a security interest, costs of administration, attorneys fees, and taxes. Therefore, you have to determine the aggregate amount of these claims to see whether there would be sufficient funds to pay the priority claims of creditors extending payment after the Chapter 11 filing if the company were liquidated.

I do not recommend extensive credit without a careful analysis by your attorney of the safety of your priority claim. Faced with this situation, many suppliers extend nominal credit (order to order) to retain the goodwill of the account and still remain consistent with the risk of extending credit to a Chapter 11 company.

13.5 YOUR RIGHTS WHEN AN ACCOUNT MAKES AN ASSIGNMENT FOR THE BENEFIT OF CREDITORS

Q. *What do we do when a customer liquidates a business under an Assignment for the Benefit of Creditors? We were just notified that one of our older customers made an assignment, but the customer still owes us over $40,000.*

A. Most states have laws that allow a business to liquidate under an Assignment for the Benefit of Creditors. Essentially, a debtor who makes an assignment transfers all property to an assignee for purposes of allowing the assignee to liquidate the assets and pay the creditors their pro rata shares of the proceeds. To this extent an assignment is very similar to a bankruptcy.

The advantage of an assignment over a bankruptcy is that the assignment is less cumbersome and in most states does not involve court supervision. Its disadvantage to creditors is that the assignee does not have the broad powers to reclaim preferential payments, as a trustee in bankruptcy would have.

You will receive an assent form from the assignee. If you believe the debtor was honest and the business can be conveniently liquidated through the assignment, you should sign the assent, approve the assignment, and simply wait for an accounting and a dividend. Creditors believing the business affairs require closer scrutiny may petition the business into bankruptcy within four months of the assignment.

In many states assignments are a more common form of insolvency liquidation than bankruptcy. It can be a very practical but frequently misunderstood way to wind up the affairs of a troubled business.

13.6 HOW TO FILE A PROOF OF CLAIM WHEN A CUSTOMER GOES BANKRUPT

Q. *One of our accounts recently filed for bankruptcy owing us over $16,000. What procedure must we follow to obtain a dividend?*

A. Creditors are required to file a proof of claim with the bankruptcy court within six months from the date of the first meeting of creditors. It's not difficult to complete a proof of claim form, and it seldom requires the assistance of an attorney. An attorney should, however, prepare claims for the following.

- Lessor under a lease
- Secured creditor
- Creditor whose debt is disputed.

Proofs of claim forms are available from the clerk of your local bankruptcy court or from legal stationers.

After all the claims are filed, the claims that are not disputed will be paid in the same manner as pro rata dividends payable to other creditors of the same class. If the debt is disputed, the court will hold a hearing to determine whether your claim should be allowed. Because that involves an adversary proceeding, it will be necessary to obtain counsel.

13.7 CAN A BANKRUPT COMPANY DISCHARGE A FRAUDULENTLY INCURRED DEBT THROUGH BANKRUPTCY

Q. *Two years ago we received a financial statement from a prospective account, and it disclosed an excellent financial* *condition. We now find that the statement was fraudulent, as the company had serious financial trouble at the time. The company has since filed for bankruptcy. Can we object to discharge of our debt?*

A. You can, but what practical purpose will it serve? A debt incurred through fraud, deceit, or misrepresentation is not dischargeable if the creditor objects.

Assume you prove your case. All it will do for you is to keep your claim alive against the corporation. Since the corporation went through bankruptcy and has no assets or business operation, your judgment will have no value. Of course, if the debtor only filed Chapter 11 or is a person instead of a corporation, then you would have practical recourse to collect the entire debt.

You should consider instead the possibility of filing suit against the principal officer who issued the fraudulent statement. An officer who commits a fraudulent act on behalf of a corporation will have personal liability for the deceit.

13.8 HOW TO PERFECT YOUR RIGHTS TO GOODS AHEAD OF EXISTING SECURED CREDITORS

Q. *We want to sell an account a $25,000 computer on credit. Our problem is that we want to secure the loan with a security interest on the computer, but a bank holds a prior security interest on all assets of the account, including equipment. How can we create a security interest on the computer that will give us first claim to it?*

A. The Uniform Commercial Code provides for this contingency. A seller financing goods or equipment sold can obtain a "purchase money" security interest on the items sold. You, as the seller, will have priority over existing security interests on the same collateral if you follow these steps.

1. Notify all existing security holders that you intend to sell specified goods (the computer) to the account and take back a purchase money security interest.

2. Notice should be in writing and be delivered within 10 days of the sale. Check state law for variances.

3. File a copy of your security interest (or financing statements) in accordance with state law, prior to delivery of the computer to the account.

A "purchase money" security interest provides a customer the opportunity to obtain further credit on a secured basis, and because existing creditors are notified as new assets come into the debtor's business to secure the "purchase money" mortgage, all parties are protected.

13.9 HOW TO BUY A SELLER'S INVENTORY FREE OF CREDITORS' CLAIMS

Q. *We operate a retail "close-out" store, and occasionally we have the opportunity to buy the inventory from retailers going out of business. How can we protect ourselves from claims of a seller's creditors?*

A. If you are buying all or substantially all of a business's inventory, then you should follow four steps.

1. Check to see whether there are any liens or encumbrances on file against the seller. They will be recorded in both the town where the business is located and the secretary of state's office. Check both locations. Don't buy unless any existing liens are discharged. This will protect you from claims of any creditor holding a valid encumbrance.

2. Unsecured creditors must have advance written notice of the sale. This is called the Bulk Sales Act. It prevents an insolvent debtor from selling out the collateral and pocketing the

proceeds. If the buyer does not obtain compliance with the Bulk Sales Act, the creditors of the seller can recover the goods in the hands of the buyer, and creditors have six months from the date of the sale (or knowledge of the sale) to do it. To comply with the Bulk Sales Act, have the seller give you a certified and notarized list of creditors. You must then notify them at least 10 days prior to the sale. The identity of the seller, buyer, and date of sale must be included, and you must also indicate that all creditors shall be paid in full. If the sale proceeds aren't sufficient to pay the creditors in full, then consult with your attorney, as very exacting notice requirements must be met. The notice must be sent through registered or certified mail. You don't have to concern yourself with the Bulk Sales Act if you are buying from a bankruptcy trustee, receiver, or assignee under an Assignment for the Benefit of Creditors, as they are all representatives of the creditors and the Bulk Sales Act has no application to their sales. Likewise, if you are buying from a secured party or lienholder who foreclosed on the seller, the Bulk Sales Act won't apply.

3. Make certain that the seller agrees to fully indemnify and render you harmless from any claims asserted by any creditor of the seller.

4. If you don't have full confidence in the seller's ability to indemnify you for creditors' claims, then in addition to the indemnity, you should "escrow" part or all of the purchase price so that you will have practical recourse under the indemnity.

If you have any questions about the solvency of the seller or if the sales price exceeds several thousand dollars, you should have an attorney handle the transaction for you. It can be substantially more expensive to defend yourself from creditors' claims than to protect yourself before you buy.

13.10 CAN A CONSUMER ASSIGN WAGES FOR THE PAYMENT OF A DEBT

Q. *One of our customers owes our auto body shop over $3,000 for repairs to his car. We told him that we would sue him unless he assigned to us his weekly wages until the debt was paid. Is this enforceable?*

A. No. The Uniform Consumer Credit Code prohibits the assignment of wages to secure or pay a debt due under a sale, lease, or loan agreement. Your customer can voluntarily elect to enter into an agreement to assign all or part of his salary to you as long as he retains the right to terminate the agreement whenever he chooses.

If you were to sue and obtain a judgment, you could garnish his wages to the extent permitted by law. Your rights to garnish wages are discussed further in question 3.10.

13.11 HOW TO PROTECT YOUR RIGHTS TO LEASED EQUIPMENT

Q. *We lease telephone systems to commercial accounts. Many of our leases provide that the lessees have the option to purchase the equipment for 10 percent of our cost upon the expiration of the lease. One of our accounts filed for bankruptcy, and the trustee in bankruptcy refuses to return to us the leased equipment. Do we have any rights to the equipment?*

A. That depends upon whether your account held its equipment under a "straight lease" or a "lease with a purchase option," which is really a conditional sale.

Under a "straight lease" the lessee has no rights to the equipment once the lease expires. If that is what your lease provides, you have a right to reclaim your equipment.

If your lease had the purchase option clause, it is treated as a conditional sale under the Uniform Commercial Code. To protect your interests in the equipment under an insolvency, you have to "perfect" your interest in the equipment by recording the lease, or financing statements, with the state and town where the lessee conducts business. Once this is recorded, you can reclaim your equipment in the hands of any third party, including a trustee in bankruptcy.

Under a straight lease you do not have to record, but it's still a good practice to file the financing statements describing the equipment and a notation that it's pursuant to a lease. It will only take a few moments to record the documents but it will accomplish the following.

1. A trustee will be prevented from inadvertently selling your equipment, as the trustee will have actual notice of the lease. Debtors often don't tell trustees that goods may belong to another party.

2. You will have absolute protection through recording. Even a straight lease can be challenged as a conditional sale, even without the option clause, if the terms of the transaction have the characteristics of a conditional sale.

If the equipment was placed on a straight lease or if you leased it as a conditional sale with proper recording, you should be successful in reclaiming the goods by having your attorney file a complaint for reclamation with the bankruptcy court. You would also have the right to file a proof of claim to obtain dividends due you as a general creditor for any damages arising from the breach of lease.

13.12   YOUR RIGHTS TO RECLAIM AND RESELL GOODS SOLD ON CONDITIONAL SALE

Q.   *Our appliance store often sells appliances on conditional sales, while reserving title to the goods until they are fully paid* *for. If a customer defaults in payment, can we reclaim the goods, resell them, and sue the customer for any deficiency?*

A. Under the Uniform Consumer Credit Code you would have to elect between two remedies if the original sale were less than $1,000. You can (1) reclaim the goods in full satisfaction of the debt or (2) not reclaim the goods and sue for the balance owed. If the sale exceeded $1,000, you can reclaim the goods, resell them in a commercially reasonable manner, and sue for any remaining deficiency, including costs and expenses.

13.13 YOUR RIGHTS TO RECLAIM GOODS FROM AN INSOLVENT CUSTOMER

Q. *As a manufacturer of sportswear we experience bad debts in excess of 3 percent of sales. Under what circumstances can we reclaim goods sold to an insolvent buyer?*

A. You have only three possibilities.

1. If you find that the buyer is insolvent while the goods are still in transit, you can stop delivery and have the goods returned to you. The only exception to this is a buyer who has a negotiable bill of lading.

2. If the buyer declares bankruptcy or otherwise institutes an insolvency proceeding (Chapter 11 reorganization, receivership, or Assignment for the Benefit of Creditors), within 10 days of receipt of your goods, you have the right to reclaim whatever merchandise may be left, making certain to give timely notice before the goods are sold or liquidated.

3. The only other situation in which you could reclaim is one in which you hold a security interest in your merchandise or have sold the merchandise on a "validly perfected" consignment basis. Refer to question 7.7 for further information on effectively securing goods sold on consignment.

Under all other circumstances you will lose all rights to the goods sold. Under the insolvency your goods will be liquidated together with all other assets, and the proceeds will be divided on a pro rata basis to the creditors.

13.14   TWELVE COLLECTION PRACTICES THAT CAN GET YOU INTO TROUBLE

Q.   With a tight economy it seems as if more people and businesses are defaulting on their payments to creditors. We want to adopt a "get tough" policy in collecting overdue accounts. How tough can we get without breaking the law?

A.   Because many creditors in the past have used some questionable tactics to collect their money, the FTC passed some stringent rules to prevent misleading or harassing tactics against debtors. Debtors also had certain common law and statutory rights against "overreaching" by creditors even before the FTC stepped in. These are the illegal tactics you'll want to know about.

1.   Never make threats of any kind, except the threat of a civil suit to collect.

2.   When writing or calling, disclose your identity. Don't pretend to be somebody else.

3.   Don't hold yourself out as a credit agency, lawyer, sheriff, or government agent (unless you are).

4.   Don't threaten a criminal action; that's extortion. And don't threaten to petition the debtor into bankruptcy, as that violates bankruptcy law.

5.   You have no right to reclaim your goods unless sold on consignment, conditional sale, or retained under a lease, but even under these conditions, if the debtor refuses you access, you cannot forceably enter or use "self-help." You'll have to go

to court to enjoin interference with your rights to reclaim the goods.

6. Don't send notices disguised as lawsuits or court documents.

7. Don't call a consumer at that consumer's place of business.

8. You are limited to calling a consumer only at home during reasonable hours.

9. You may not start suit in a state other than that in which the debtor is located unless the debtor physically incurred the debt in that state.

10. Never send notices of default on a postcard or have your envelope indicate that the contents relate to a collection effort. Likewise, don't discuss the account in the presence of a third party.

11. You can refer the delinquency to a credit reporting agency, but don't notify other creditors or suppliers.

12. Don't deviate from customary and accepted collection practices. Become too aggressive and you may find yourself on the defensive rather than the offensive.

CHAPTER
14

Protecting Your Business From Creditors

14.1 HOW TO SETTLE WITH CREDITORS FOR A FRACTION ON THE DOLLAR

Q. *We owe general creditors over $200,000 and are experiencing serious financial difficulty in our restaurant supply firm. How can we negotiate a settlement with the creditors without going through the "red tape" of a bankruptcy proceeding?*

A. Distressed businesses often first try a "composition" agreement with creditors. The approach may differ from situation to situation, but here's the technique that I've found best.

1. Calculate what the creditors would receive if your business did fail. An appraiser would have to ascertain the value of your assets at auction to arrive at the dollar amount that would be available to creditors.

2. Subtract debts that would have to be paid first and give these priority over those of the general creditors. They should include

- Secured debts
- Accrued wages
- Taxes (federal, state, and local)

This will show you what the general creditors are likely to receive if the business does fail, which it may if they do go along with any reasonable settlement you propose.

3. Convene a meeting of several of your largest creditors. Be candid and give them the facts. Be prepared to tell them why the business ran into trouble, its future prospects, what they would receive if the business does fail, and why your offer is reasonable. Logically, you will have to offer something more than they could receive under a bankruptcy.

4. Be certain that you can perform under your negotiated settlement. It may be an immediate payment for a fraction of their claims, payment of the entire amount over an extended period, or a combination of the two. I don't recommend a settlement that exceeds what the business can pay over a three- to four-year period, as anything beyond that only encumbers your own future.

5. Once you negotiate a settlement with the creditors' committee, the committee can then "sell" your plan to the smaller creditors. Usually the plan will be conditional upon acceptance by a certain percentage of your creditors (80 to 90 percent).

Structuring a settlement with creditors always involves the elements of accounting, law, and common negotiating strategy. That's why you must involve your accountant and attorney before you approach your creditors.

The one problem with a composition agreement is that it admits insolvency. If you are unable to negotiate a settlement with your creditors, you may be required to try more drastic steps to reduce liabilities and protect the business. In most cases the distressed business will then file for reorganization under Chapter 11, which will protect the business while it continues to negotiate a fair settlement with its creditors.

For smaller companies a composition agreement should be attempted first, as it may achieve the same results with substantially less cost, risk, and effort. Always make certain that your attorney drafts the composition agreement, as you want to make certain that your creditors remain bound on the settlement.

14.2   DEFENSES YOU SHOULD CONSIDER TO A CREDITOR'S CLAIM

Q. *What defenses to nonpayment for goods sold are generally available? We have plenty of problems with our suppliers, and many of our bills are long overdue, with creditors pressing for payment.*

A. The list is extensive and includes basic contract defenses as well as any defenses you may have under the Uniform Commercial Code. From my experiences in defending against creditors' claims I have found the following defenses to be the most common.

1. *Defective goods:* This can be an affirmative defense to nonpayment, but to solidify your defense, you should give the seller timely notice of the defects (see question 6.3 for the procedures to follow).

2. *Price not in conformity with contract:* Price disagreements do happen. Purchase orders should also be complete as to price; otherwise you may be bound to the seller's most recent price list, even though it exceeds what you expected to pay for the goods.

3. *Prior payment:* This generally happens when you have ongoing transactions with a seller and disagree as to the remaining balance owed. Only a proper reconciliation of accounts can untangle this properly.

4. *Return goods:* You do not have the right to return goods unless you expressly purchased the goods on these terms. A sales representative will often imply this right, but the seller won't honor it. If you do buy with the right to return, make certain that clause is in your contract, purchase order, or invoice.

5. *Statute of limitations:* On claims arising from goods sold, a creditor only has four years (in most states) to commence suit. The four years begin to run either from the date payment was due or from the date of your last payment or written acknowledgment of the obligation.

All too often debtors overlook common defenses. If you have any dispute or problem with a supplier, review all the facts with your counsel. An attorney may be able to find valid defenses that you never knew about.

14.3 WHAT A CHAPTER 11 REORGANIZATION CAN DO FOR YOU

Q. *In this depressed economy we hear of more and more businesses filing for reorganization under Chapter 11 of the Bankruptcy Code. Can you give me a brief outline of what Chapter 11 can do for these companies?*

A. Many firms that would otherwise fail because of oppressive debts and contracts seek protection in the federal bankruptcy courts while they attempt to restructure their financial affairs. Chapter 11 affords the debtor sweeping rights to regain financial solvency and stay in business. A company in Chapter 11 can do the following.

1. It can freeze all its past debts and is protected from further prosecution from creditors' suits while attempting to negotiate a settlement with the creditors. What the creditors may eventually settle for will depend on their position if the business failed and the process of negotiation. In many cases creditors will accept as little as 5 or 10 cents on the dollar depending on the economics of the situation.

2. It can stop secured creditors or mortgage holders from foreclosing without further approval of the court. In some instances the total secured debt can even be reduced through the reorganization.

3. It can stop the IRS and other taxing authorities from seizing business assets to satisfy past tax claims.

4. It can allow the business to terminate burdensome or unprofitable leases, contracts, and even employment agreements.

5. It can provide the business an increased opportunity to refinance or to obtain new credit.

6. It can issue new shares of stock to raise further equity capital.

As you can see, these and other benefits of a Chapter 11 can give most businesses that deserve to stay in business a fresh start free from most of the problems and mistakes of the past. Handled by experienced counsel, the continuity of the business will be of greater benefit to creditors and the debtor than would a bankruptcy or other liquidation.

14.4   YOU CAN STOP SECURED CREDITORS FROM FORECLOSING

Q.   *We owe a local bank over $100,000 and are delinquent by three months in our payments. The bank is threatening foreclosure on the chattel mortgage (security agreement). Do they have to go to court to foreclose, and what can we do to stop them?*

A.   A secured lender does not have to go to court to foreclose, as no court involvement is necessary. Here are the steps the lender must take.

1. The lender must notify you of the intent to foreclose. This letter should spell out what's owed, why the loan is in default, and when the lender will take possession of the collateral. The notice should also tell you your rights to pay the note and stop the foreclosure.

2. The lender must then take actual physical possession of the collateral. A lender can take whatever steps are necessary to protect it, and this may mean either removing it or padlocking the entire premises if the collateral consists of virtually all your assets.

3. The next step is to advertise the collateral for sale. The lender must notify you of the day and place for any intended sale so that you can be present to protect your interests. The security agreement will often specify the amount of time that must transpire before the sale.

4. The collateral must be sold in a "commercially reasonable" manner. This means either a public auction conducted by a qualified auctioneer and reasonable advertising of the sale or a private sale without auction. If it's a private sale, the lender will establish by appraisal that the price received is in excess of what could be obtained by public auction.

5. You have the right to stop the foreclosure any time prior to the sale by paying the loan in full, including costs and attorneys' fees. Upon sale, however, you lose all rights to the collateral.

6. If the sale generates a surplus over the loan, you will receive that surplus. If it brings less, you will be liable for the deficiency, and the lender will then be an unsecured creditor.

Following are practical steps to take that may be successful in stopping the foreclosure.

1. Negotiate with the lender. Foreclosure should only come about if you can't convince the lender that the business can't pay the loan or that the lender's position will be jeopardized by not foreclosing on the collateral. A reasonable payment plan and assurance that you will maintain the collateral value can be a convincing argument.

2. If negotiating a loan extension doesn't work, try to convince the lender to sell only part of the collateral to the extent necessary to pay the loan. For example, it doesn't make sense to sink a business by foreclosing on $100,000 worth of collateral if you only owe the lender $10,000. Why not isolate excess assets, receivables, or little-used equipment to satisfy the $10,000 and allow the business to survive?

3. You may have legal defenses to the foreclosure. If you can raise any legal defense to the loan or the loan balance (disagreement as to what's owed, misrepresentation, breach of contract, etc.), your attorney may be able to restrain the foreclosure in court.

4. When all else fails, you can try a Chapter 11 reorganization under the Bankruptcy Code. If you file before the collat-

eral is sold, the lender will have to stop its foreclosure proceedings and give you back the collateral. The lender can then petition the bankruptcy court for permission to foreclose, and the decision will be based on who will incur the greater loss if the foreclosure is or is not allowed to proceed.

A secured party is always in a strong position as long as you have enough collateral to cover the loan. For this reason you should always give priority to these creditors and keep their loans current, even when you do have a cash flow problem.

14.5 CAN A SECURED PARTY RETAIN THE COLLATERAL

Q. *Our firm financed the purchase of an $18,000 computer by borrowing from a finance company and securing the loan with a mortgage on the computer. We paid the loan down to $8,000 and defaulted. Upon our default, the finance company foreclosed on the computer and stored it in a warehouse. Aren't they obligated to sell it?*

A. Yes. A secured party must resell the collateral. If the proceeds are less than what's owed, you would be liable for the deficiency. If there was a surplus, you would be entitled to receive it. Without a sale you have no way to determine whether there would be a deficiency or a surplus.

A secured party has the duty not only to sell the collateral but also to sell it in a commercially reasonable manner. This implies the duty to sell it within a reasonable time and without incurring needless costs. Delayed storage in a warehouse satisfies neither requirement. Note, however, two exceptions to the requirement to resell.

1. The debtor agrees to retention of the collateral in full satisfaction of the claim.

2. The goods are sold for $1,000 or less on conditional sale. In this instance the creditor can elect to retain the goods as full discharge of the debt.

You would have the right to compel the sale by seeking a court order. You may also have a valid defense to a deficiency claim based on the improper conduct by the secured party.

14.6 CAN A CREDITOR RECLAIM GOODS

Q. *Our firm purchased $15,000 in electrical equipment from a supplier, and because of poor sales, we are unable to pay the bill. The supplier phoned and told me that unless we paid within the next week he'd show up with a truck and take the goods back. Can he do that?*

A. Not without your permission. Once a creditor sells you goods, you have title. The creditor loses all claim to the goods sold and can only sue you for the purchase price. The only exceptions are goods sold on consignment, conditional sale, or otherwise secured by a security agreement.

Chances are that your supplier knows that he doesn't have the authority to reclaim his goods. He may be trying to scare you into payment, or perhaps he believes you don't know your rights and will voluntarily give him back the goods.

Threatening to take back "unpaid" goods is an increasingly common tactic by creditors. One credit manager reports that 20 to 30 percent of customers don't realize that the supplier cannot legally reclaim goods and therefore they allow suppliers to come in and pick them up.

Should your supplier try forceably to remove the goods from your premises, you can treat this as trespassing and use reasonable force to remove him from the premises.

14.7 COMMON ERRORS THAT CAN MAKE YOU LIABLE FOR CORPORATE OBLIGATIONS

Q. *A supplier sold my corporation $7,000 worth of goods, and the supplier is now suing me personally for payment and claiming that I am liable. How can I be liable for the corporation's debt if I never guaranteed the bill?*

A. You cannot be personally liable on the debt as a guarantor unless the guarantee is in writing, as the guarantee to pay the debts of another (your corporation) must be reduced to writing to be enforceable.

Through billing errors, however, suppliers often send invoices to individuals rather than to corporations and then try to assert a claim as an individual obligation. Here are several important steps you can take to make certain that obligations remain only those of the corporation.

1. Never order goods under your personal name. Your purchase orders and sales contracts should always be under the name of the corporation.

2. Reject any invoices billed to you personally. Notify the supplier to rebill properly by using the corporate name.

3. Don't pay corporate debts with personal checks. This can create confusion as to the party the supplier is really dealing with.

4. If you incorporate your business, notify all creditors in writing of the incorporation and note that all future shipments shall be to the corporation.

5. Always sign agreements, checks, notes, and other corporate documents clearly showing your agency capacity. For example, these documents might properly be signed

XYZ Company, Inc.
By John Jones, President

If you simply sign as John Jones, you can be personally bound as the document doesn't clearly show you are acting on behalf of the corporation.

Unfortunately, even when it's clear that the corporation is liable, many creditors will try to find an excuse to sue you personally, particularly if your corporation is insolvent. If you are properly defended, they have no chance of collecting, but your creditor may be gambling on the possibility that you will accept the liability or default in your defense.

Although you can't stop the few lawsuits that may be misdirected to you, you can escape liability by following these points.

14.8   YOUR RIGHTS TO CONTEST YOUR CREDIT RATING

Q.   *Several prospective suppliers have informed us that our credit rating is poor. We have a dispute with two creditors, and they may have submitted an adverse credit report to the credit bureau. What can we do to correct the record?*

A.   Every debtor has the following rights relative to a credit report. You can do any of the following.

1. Demand the name of the credit bureau or reporting agency issuing the report.

2. Insist on seeing a copy of your credit report.

3. File all documents or written responses to point out disputed claims and ask that they be made part of the record.

4. Request that incorrect entries be deleted or issue a statement of your position on any matter you consider incorrect.

5. Ask past creditors whose claims are satisfied to withdraw any adverse report filed on you, although this is discretionary with your creditor.

Perhaps the best way to convince a supplier that you are credit worthy is to approach the supplier directly and explain any adverse entries in your credit report. Suppliers know that disputes can arise and that a credit report does not always represent the most accurate picture.

14.9 WHAT YOUR CREDITORS CAN RECOVER FROM YOU IF YOUR BUSINESS GOES BANKRUPT

Q. *My publishing corporation is insolvent, and filing for bankruptcy appears to be the only salvation. When I started the business, I loaned it $100,000, and over the past two years I've repaid myself $50,000 on these loans. In addition I have paid myself a $50,000 annual salary for each of the past two years. If I do put the corporation into bankruptcy, will the creditors have any claim against me?*

A. Yes. As a principal in the corporation you are considered an "insider." Any payments made to an insider on past obligations is a voidable preference to the extent paid within one year from the date you file the bankruptcy. Anything you repaid yourself more than one year ago is safe. Therefore, the trustee in bankruptcy could sue you for all loan repayments you made to yourself within the prior year.

Your salary may be another problem. Salaries far in excess of reasonable compensation can be challenged as a "fraudulent transfer." Generally, the trustee will only consider such excess payments during the prior year.

Your strategy should be to try to keep your business *out* of bankruptcy for one year from the date of your last note repayment. Then you'll be safe from any claim.

These same rules apply even if you file for protection under Chapter 11 of the Bankruptcy Code for purposes of reorganizing your company. The creditors can demand that you repay the corporation any preferential payment made to yourself within one year prior to the filing.

14.10   SUREFIRE WAYS TO AVOID TROUBLE WITH CREDITORS IF YOU DO FAIL

Q. *Our problem is our poor financial condition. We have such a poor credit rating that it's difficult to obtain credit. Some suppliers won't bother to check our credit rating, but we want to avoid legal problems in obtaining merchandise under these circumstances. What precautions should we take?*

A. Many companies are in just your position. They need credit to survive and can get into a lot of trouble if they obtain it the wrong way. Here are the problem areas.

1. Never issue a false financial statement or give misleading information about your company. You may be tempted to "fudge" the credit application, but it can cause serious problems. The creditor can contest the discharge of the debt in bankruptcy as being fraudulently incurred, and what's worse is that you can be liable criminally for mail fraud. The creditor can even sue you personally for deceit.

2. Don't buy merchandise on credit unless you have at least a reasonable expectation of paying for it. If the creditor can prove you ordered it without any expectation of payment, you could have serious criminal problems.

3. If you do receive merchandise on credit, never sell it in "wholesale lots" or "back door" it. It should only be sold in the ordinary course of business; otherwise it's bankruptcy fraud should your business fail.

4. Keep adequate books and records. If your business does fail, you want to provide your creditors with complete accountability. Your ability to prove that you have operated your

business in an honest way will shield you from legal entanglements.

5. Don't issue "bad checks" for COD or partially prepaid orders. If a creditor relies on your check to make shipment, you may face criminal violations if your check bounces.

6. If you own several stores, each operating as a separate corporation, then avoid shipments between stores. Creditors often claim that goods have been transferred to another store before the store that actually purchased it went bankrupt. If you do sell any merchandise to another store, document the transaction carefully and have it verified by an employee.

CHAPTER
15

Other Problems,
Other Solutions

15.1 AVOIDING LIABILITY WHEN GIVING CREDIT REFERENCES

Q. *As a drug wholesaler, we often are requested to give credit information on our accounts from other suppliers. In fact a few of our late-paying accounts have asked us whether we would give "favorable" references to new suppliers. What's our liability in this situation?*

A. Liability arising from erroneous or improper credit reporting can be serious and can come from any one of several directions. For example, if you provide a supplier with a "good" reference for an obviously delinquent customer, you could be liable for deceit, and in some states you may even have to pay double or treble damages under a "deceptive trade practices" statute.

Likewise, if you make improper statements about a customer, you could incur liability to the customer for libel or interference with contractual rights. Finally, if you meet with competitors to discuss credit and the financial conditions of the accounts you have in common or to freely exchange credit information, it might be construed as a boycott in violation of the Sherman Act of the antitrust laws. Take this approach.

1. Stick to the facts in giving credit information. If an account is running 90 days late, say so. Don't categorize the account with damaging adjectives (deadbeat, never pays bills, or even slow pay). Allow the person obtaining the reference to draw individual conclusions from the hard facts you provide.

2. If a customer contests liability to you, this should be communicated. Put the total credit history in a full perspective.

3. You can decline to give any credit information. That is

your prerogative, not your customer's. Many companies now follow that policy for all accounts.

4. Don't exchange credit information with competitors under the guise of a credit association.

5. Never falsify or distort the credit picture. You will have the same liability as your customer.

15.2 CAN YOUR COMPANY BE LIABLE FOR COMPUTER ERROR

Q. *Through a technical problem in our computer programming our computer erroneously submitted negative credit information concerning one of our better accounts. The account now threatens to sue us. Are we liable?*

A. Computers can be as fallible as humans. Although there are very few cases involving computer error, it's reasonably safe to conclude that you would not have liability.

To maintain an action against you for defamation (the erroneous credit report), the customer would have to show that the report was maliciously issued. An adverse error made through common negligence would not be sufficient. Of course, you do have the obligation to correct or mitigate any damage caused by issuing a corrected report and a full explanation for the prior error.

In some cases a computer has erroneously issued a statement showing an owed balance below the actual amount due. The customer will then try to defend against the claim for payment by pointing to the prior computer statement. In these instances the courts routinely disregard the erroneous statement upon a showing of technical error and validation of the rightful amount due.

As long as we have computers, it will be inevitable that we will have errors. As with human error you will have little problem as long as you can detect error within a reasonable time and take immediate steps to rectify it.

15.3 THE RIGHTS TO LOST OR MISPLACED PROPERTY FOUND IN YOUR PLACE OF BUSINESS

Q. *One of our customers found another customer's wallet on the floor in our tavern. We demanded that she turn it over to us in case its owner returned, but she refused, claiming that she was entitled to it because she found it. Did we have the right to demand it?*

A. No. If lost property is found in a public place under such circumstances that a customer lost, rather than misplaced, the item, the finder would have better rights to it than the proprietor of the business. If the item, such as a hat, coat, or briefcase was misplaced or unintentionally left behind, then the proprietor can demand it on the expectation the customer will return for it.

Even where property is lost and the finder turns it over to the proprietor with the hope that the customer will return, the proprietor only holds it in trust for the person who lost the item. If the customer does not return, the finder can usually claim the item. Local law should be consulted, as many states have strict time requirements on reclaiming lost or misplaced goods.

15.4 WHEN YOU CANNOT DISCLAIM LIABILITY

Q. *Can we "disclaim" liability for damage to a customer's car while it's parked in our parking lot? We have printed on* *our parking stubs a disclaimer stating that "we shall not be liable for damage, theft, or loss to the vehicle or any of its contents."*

A. Ticket stub disclaimers are generally not an effective way to avoid liability. The courts have ruled that this type of disclaimer is not sufficiently conspicuous to be noticed by the customer and that any such disclaimer is against public policy as an attempt to relieve yourself of common law liability that does exist.

If your customers park and lock their cars, you may be able to avoid liability by claiming that your customers did not put their vehicles under your control; you only allowed the use of space. Clearly, you would have less liability in this situation.

You can legally limit liability if you adequately post the limitation and the disclaimer is reasonable. For example, posting a sign stating that the customer is to lock the car may shift'the burden to the customer if the car is stolen. Likewise, notices that no attendant shall be on duty after a stated hour and that all cars are to be removed by that time would be an equally valid defense to damage to a car left after hours.

You have nothing to lose by continuing the disclaimer. Even though its enforceability is questionable, many customers believe they are legally bound by it and don't challenge it.

15.5 ARE YOUR ADS MISLEADING

Q. *As a small firm, we have developed some new products and after local test marketing want to start an extensive direct mail campaign for national sales. What does the FTC consider deceptive or misleading advertising, as we want to avoid legal entanglements?*

A. You have more than the FTC to worry about. Consumer agencies in every state are also on the lookout for deceptive ads, and because you will be using the mails to ship your product, you also have postal regulations to contend with. To stay on the right side of the law, follow these guidelines.

1. Don't make specific statements or representations unless you can back them with scientific tests or other proof that the statements are true. You can use such "selling expressions" as "valuable," "efficient," or "excellent," as these terms do not express a statement of fact.

2. Don't advertise your product as "new" if it's more than six months old.

3. Don't imply that your product had a country of origin unless it was actually produced in that country. You can say, for example, that your American-made sunglasses are "French inspired" or that your Brooklyn-made shoes are "Italian design."

4. Endorsements must be handled carefully. Don't suggest the product is endorsed by any group unless you have that endorsement in writing, and then duplicate the entire recommendation so that the consumer doesn't read a distorted blurb.

5. Avoid use of a company or brand name that could cause the consumer to think you or your product is associated with another company.

6. Don't advertise a limited supply unless your supply is short. The FTC takes the position that this places undue pressure on the consumer.

7. Don't compare your product with a competitor's unless you give a full and fair comparison of all relevant points.

8. Don't say that your product can accomplish a specific purpose unless the product can reasonably serve that purpose without special skill or need to buy additional items.

9. If your product is sold on credit, you will also have to comply with the Federal Truth in Lending Act. Question 13.1 will show you how to comply with its provisions.

10. Check every word in your ad. Put yourself in the position of a prospective customer and ask yourself, "Would I know exactly what I am buying, and does my product measure up to that expectation?"

If you are dealing with an ad agency, it undoubtedly will screen your ad for obvious deceptions. But don't rely entirely on the agency. You have the primary responsibility to ensure honest advertising.

15.6   AVOIDING SERIOUS ANTITRUST VIOLATIONS

Q.   *We are one of only five wholesale plumbing firms in our city, and as part of a small industry, we work closely with the other firms. Generally, we watch the prices being charged by the largest supplier and then change our prices to duplicate theirs. Is this illegal?*

A.   In antitrust language what you are doing is called "conscious price parallelism." You have the right to observe the pricing policies of a competitor and respond by changing your own, even if you end up with identical price structures.

What is illegal is any agreement or arrangement whereby you and at least one of your competitors mutually decide on a pricing structure. Here are other agreements that are prohibited.

- Agreements between competitors to restrict territories or to allocate customers
- Agreements between competitors on credit, shipping, or return of goods policies
- Agreements between competitors on cash or trade discounts, advertising, promotional allowances, or other sales inducements
- Agreements between competitors or with other customers to boycott either a supplier or customer.

In fact, there are so many prohibitions on undertakings between competitors that a simple but safe rule of thumb to follow is never to discuss or agree on any policy relating to your operation.

15.7 YOU CAN BE LIABLE FOR STATEMENTS CONCERNING A SUPPLIER'S PRODUCT

Q. *Our firm belongs to a buying "cooperative" containing 50 participating hardware stores. We have just received a shipment of goods from an importer. They are to be used in a cooperative promotional program, and the other stores will soon receive their shipments. The merchandise is defective and of very poor quality. Can we notify the other stores about the problem so that they can refuse the goods before shipment and payment?*

A. You may have a problem if you do. The general rule is that any derogatory remark or statement about the product or business of another can result in an action for defamation or slander of title.

You may have a "qualified privilege" to make the statement, as you would be making the statement to other parties with a corresponding interest in the quality of the product. It follows the same rule of privilege that allows a credit bureau to issue reports to members with apparent immunity.

If you do feel an obligation to report your dissatisfaction with the product to member stores, you should not categorize the products as "poor," "inferior," or "defective," but instead you should refer to your findings on the specifications by saying, for example, "Six out of nine items have a broken stem." In this manner you are only reporting observable facts without dangerous product characterization. Your members will get the message, and your objective will be safely accomplished.

Making a derogatory or defamatory statement about another's business, product, or service to one with no apparent interest would create greater liability, as you no longer have a "qualified privilege." This is particularly true when you make the statement in writing, for unlike spoken slander of title, the plaintiff would not have to prove actual damages.

15.8   YOUR LIABILITY IN INTERFERING WITH EXISTING CONTRACTS

Q.   *Our firm operates a wholesale food commissary by selling primarily to canteen trucks. Several canteen drivers have "purchasing" contracts with a competing wholesaler, but because our prices are lower, they want to switch their accounts to us. Would we have any liability if we accept them as customers?*

A.   You would if you knew of the existing contracts and induced the canteen drivers to break their contract so that they could buy from you. You could be sued for interference with contractual rights and be liable for all profits your competitor lost.

Interference with existing contractual relationships is actionable regardless of the type of contract. For example, it would also extend to your inducing a prospective employee to terminate an employment contract to work for you. Generally, you do not have liability under the following conditions.

1. No existing contract existed, but the relationship could be terminated at will without constituting a breach. That's why you can freely compete for new accounts that don't have a binding commitment to another supplier.

2. You had no knowledge of the contract or played no part in inducing your account to break it.

My recommendation to you would be to have the canteen drivers sign an acknowledgment that they are buying from you without any inducement on your part. Make the facts conform. Don't interfere with your competitor's contracts unless you want to defend a lawsuit. Your best strategy may be simply to wait for the contracts to expire and then take over the accounts without problems.

15.9   YOU MAY BE LIABLE FOR THE CRIMINAL ACTS OF YOUR CORPORATION

Q.   *If my corporation commits a criminal act, can I, as its president, be held criminally liable?*

A.   Your liability would depend on the nature of the criminal act, the provisions of the statute, and whether you had acknowledged, approved, or condoned the illegal activity. The general rule is that a corporate entity will not shield an individual committing an illegal act. Participation, prior approval, or ratification of the act will in most instances make you an accessory if not a principal defendant in the criminal proceeding.

In some instances court cases have held a principal officer criminally liable for the illegal acts of the corporation even when the officer has no knowledge of the criminal wrongdoing. Most of these cases involved Food and Drug Act violations, and violations of the antitrust and FTC laws.

An officer can usually be liable for bad check charges even when signing the check in a representative capacity. Such liability is based on the officer's knowledge of the availability of funds to pay checks at the time of issue.

Prosecutors and courts alike tend to assess criminal responsibility on the responsible officers when they can show that the officer had imputed knowledge. It may be that you did not realize that subordinates were subjecting the corporation to a criminal act, but if you had the reasonable ability to foresee the act and could have taken timely action to prevent it, you could be liable.

The best defense to personal involvement in a corporate crime is to demonstrate that you have taken all reasonable steps to prevent it. Consider these practical guidelines.

1. Make certain that your operations policy states operative rules that fully comply with all laws.

2. Never encourage or condone illegal activities by employees.

3. If you do discover an illegal act, reprimand or terminate the involved employees and take all steps to correct the illegality.

4. Serious crimes should be reported to the authorities. Failure to do so can make you an accessory to the crime.

It's not common for the government to prosecute an officer who has no personal complicity in the corporate crime if the officer can show that personal conduct was consistent with a policy of compliance.

15.10   WHEN NOT TO TALK TO GOVERNMENT AGENTS

Q.   Can you provide some guidance as to when a business person should refuse to talk to a government or law enforcement agent?

A.   The average business person walks a fine line in making that determination. On one hand business people want to cooperate and avoid the appearance of wrongdoing, but on the other they know that what they say may incriminate them. From my experiences 30 to 40 percent of all convictions against business people come about because they did make damaging admissions. I suggest you never talk to a government agent under the following situations.

1. *A visit by a special agent of the IRS:* Special agents investigate criminal tax fraud cases. If a revenue officer does call on you, ask for identification, which the officer is obligated to show you.

2. *An OSHA inspector showing up with a search warrant* If OSHA officials obtained a search warrant in advance, they suspect serious problems.

3. *Your having been read your "rights" under the "Miranda" ruling:* Once given this warning, you are forewarned that you are suspected of a crime, and that's the time to remain silent.

4. *Any audit or inspection that you do not consider customary or ordinary:* Should you be involved in any extraordinary investigation or have any enforcement agent appear with a search warrant, it's best to remain silent.

5. *Any arrest or service upon you of any criminal process:* Always consult an attorney before discussing anything.

Faced with any of these situations, you should refuse any comment and immediately call your counsel. You are never required to talk to a law enforcement or government agent. You can decline to answer any questions or stop at any time. You also have the right to refer the agent to your counsel or ask the agent to leave your premises unless a valid search warrant has been presented.

Don't be afraid to assert your rights. This can protect you against damaging admissions that can be used against you at a later date.

15.11 KNOW THE RIGHT WAY TO MAKE POLITICAL CONTRIBUTIONS

Q. *We operate a politically sensitive business. To what extent can our corporation make political contributions?*

A. These are the guidelines to follow.

1. Your corporation *cannot* make any contribution to a federal election. Federal law prevents this for any size of corporation.

2. You *can* have your employees set up an independent "political action fund." They can donate to the fund and the fund, operated by a committee elected from employee ranks, can donate any amount to the candidates of their choice. The key is to keep the fund segregated from corporate funds; this is common practice with large corporations, but with smaller companies it's easier to encourage employees to make direct contributions.

3. State law *may* allow corporate contributions for state elections. Check the law in your state or obtain a letter from the candidate's committee attesting to the legality of a corporate contribution.

4. You can encourage (but not coerce or threaten) employees to donate to certain political candidates.

Corporate contributions, where legal, are generally tax deductible as a business expense.

15.12 YOUR OBLIGATIONS UNDER OSHA LAW

Q. *As a medium-sized manufacturing plant with 100 employees, we are concerned about compliance with OSHA requirements. Summarily, what are we required to do to comply with this law?*

A. As with all federal regulations they're long and complicated, and I suggest you receive a copy of the *OSHA Handbook for Small Businesses* (U.S. Publication No. 2209). Here are its major points.

1. You cannot discharge an employee for failure or refusal to work if he or she reasonably believes the premises are unsafe. Further, it's illegal to fire or discriminate against an employee because of a filed OSHA complaint.

2. It's a criminal offense to commit a welfare violation that causes an employee's death.

3. You must file a report with OSHA whenever there is an accident that causes the death of an employee or the hospitalization of five or more employees.

4. You must keep a log of OSHA injuries. This includes not only the details of work-induced injuries but even reported health problems believed to be caused by working conditions. This log has to be placed at each location. With the log is a "supplementary record" of occupational injuries and illnesses. That amplifies the details of each injury contained in the log. (These record-keeping requirements do not apply to businesses with fewer than 10 employees.)

5. You must conspicuously post the OSHA bulletins advising your workers that your plant is covered under OSHA and advising them of their rights as employees. OSHA will provide these posters.

15.13 YOUR RIGHTS IN AN OSHA INSPECTION

Q. *We suspect that an employee who was recently injured on the job notified OSHA. What can we expect if we are inspected?*

A. As with all government involvement you can expect plenty of irritation. Here's how it will go.

1. Your inspector probably won't have a search warrant, and you can insist on one. Courts routinely issue them, but it will give you time to get things in order.

2. The first step will be an "opening conference," during which the inspector will check your records. You have the right to ask whether an employee initiated the inspection, but you cannot fire or discipline the employee because of it.

3. The inspection will always be in your presence, and the inspector may invite one or two other employees on the "walk-through."

4. If the inspector tests air samples or noise levels, you should conduct your own tests to defend against the findings.

5. At the closing conference the inspector will disclose any problems. Serious problems can result in an immediate shutdown. Minor infractions usually result in nothing more than a spoken caution. Most violations can result in fines up to $1,000 for each offense, and you will be required to correct each offense within an abatement period upon notice to OSHA. You may be able to obtain an extension of the abatement period for good cause.

6. Once you receive a citation from OSHA, you have 15 days to object to it and start the appeal process, so the involvement of your attorney at that point is essential.

7. Appeals are first heard by an administrative law judge assigned to OSHA. Further appeals are heard by the U.S. Court of Appeals.

GLOSSARY

A

Acceleration.   Speeding up the due date of commercial paper.

Acceptance.   Agreeing to be bound by the terms of a bill or exchange. Also agreeing to the terms of an "offer" in a contract setting.

Accord and satisfaction.   The tender of substitute performance, which is accepted by the other party, in a contract situation.

Acknowledgment.   A formal statement attesting to the genuineness of a document or signature. Usually performed by a notary.

Affidavit.   A formal written statement made under oath.

Agency.   A relationship in which a "principal" grants specified authority to an "agent."

Assign.   To set over some legal right to another.

Assignee.   The one to whom an assignment is made.

Assignor.   The one who makes an assignment.

Attachment.   A legal step used to "tie up" something that is usually in the hands of another. For example, a wage attachment.

Attestation.   The result of acknowledging or placing a seal on a document.

B

Bait and switch.   An unscrupulous business practice that results in selling inferior merchandise or forcing the buyer to pay higher prices to get better-quality merchandise.

Bankruptcy.   A federal law that permits a systematic distribution of the assets of an insolvent debtor.

Barter.   To trade in kind or to exchange an item for something else.

Bearer paper.   A negotiable instrument that can be negotiated without any endorsement.

Beneficiary.   One who gains an ultimate benefit, as in a trust.

Bill of exchange (draft).   One of the four types of commercial paper under the Uniform Commercial Code.

Bill of sale.   A legal document listing the items of personal property sold by one to another.

Blue-sky laws.   State and federal laws designed to regulate the issuance of stocks and bonds.

Bond.   In criminal law, a document binding one to a sum of money to assure the appearance of another. Bail.

Business wrongs.   Torts committed in the business setting.

Buy-and-sell agreement.   Widely used in partnerships to spell out how one partner can buy out another.

Bylaws.   The rules of conduct of a corporation.

C

Caveat emptor.   Let the buyer beware.

Caveat venditor.   Let the seller beware.

Certificate of deposit.   One of the four types of commercial paper. Used as a savings device.

Certificate of incorporation.   A grant of powers by a state to a corporation. Frequently called a "charter."

Chattel.   An item of personal property.

Check.   One of the four types of commercial paper under the Uniform Commercial Code.

Civil action.   Private litigation between persons or firms.

Coercion.   Forcing someone into something against his or her will.

Collateral.   In secured transactions, personal property given as security for a loan.

Proceeds of collateral.   Funds realized from the sale of secured personal property.

Products of collateral.   Secured personal property that is used to create new property. For example, secured lumber used to construct kitchen cabinets.

Comingling.   Mixing up or joining so as to lose former identity. For example, coal of A and B dumped into a common coal tipple.

Commercial paper.   The subject of Article 3 of the Uniform Commercial Code.

Compensatory damages.   A monetary award to compensate one for an injury or other loss.

Competency.   Full legal capacity.

Compromise and settlement.   Adjusting and paying off a disputed claim or matter.

Consideration.   In contract law, the "reason for enforcing promises."

Consignor.   One who consigns goods.

Contract.   An agreement.

Bilateral contract.   An agreement based upon mutual promises.

Express contract.   A stated agreement.

Implied contract in fact.   An agreement assumed because of the acts of parties in dealing with each other.

Implied contract in law.   A fiction used by the courts in which the court finds an agreement where none exists.

Oral contract.   An agreement that arises from spoken words only.

Sales contract.   An agreement between merchants for the purchase and sale of goods of all types.

Written contract.   An agreement that is written or typed.

Unilateral contract.   An agreement in which one makes a promise in exchange for an act of the other party.

Conversion.   Wrongfully to appropriate the personal property of another.

D

Debentures.   Unsecured bonds.

Deceit.   An underhanded, unscrupulous action.

Deed.   A legal document widely used to convey real estate.

Default.   To break terms of an agreement.

Deficiency judgment.   A court order for a sum of money yet owing on an obligation.

Degree of proof.   The extent of evidence required in court.

Detriment.   Loss, lack of benefit, or harm suffered by one because of something done by another.

Directors.   Those who run a corporation.

Disclaim.   To deny responsibility, as for warranties.

Disclosure statement.   A form required under Truth in Lending and R.E.S.P.S. Contains prescribed matters.

Dissolution.   To dissolve or break up or the act of doing such things.

Dividend.   A division of corporate funds, usually profits.

Cash dividend.   A dividend paid by cash or check.

Ex dividend.   Without dividend.

Liquidating dividend.   A return of capital assets. Not a true dividend.

Property dividend.   A division of the products of a corporation.

Stock dividend.   A capitalization of earnings evidenced by new certificates.

Drawee. The one on whom a bill of exchange or check is drawn.

Drawer. The one who draws a bill of exchange or check.

Due process. A phrase generally understood to mean "full protection of our laws and unqualified access to our courts."

Duress. A condition of mental stress created by threats or other pressure.

E

Embezzlement. The taking of another's money which is lawfully in that person's posession, with the intention of permanently depriving the other of it.

Employment contract. An agreement between an employer and employee. Covers wages, duties, and the like.

Endorsement. Commercial paper, Article 3, of the Uniform Commercial Code. The act of signing one's name with or without additional words.

Blank endorsement. A signature only.

Qualified endorsement. A signature accompanied by qualifying words.

Restrictive endorsement. A statement limiting the use of commercial paper. For example, "for deposit only."

Special endorsement. An endorsement accompanied by the name of another person to whom the instrument is to be paid.

Endorser. One who endorses.

Endowment. In life insurance a policy payable in whole or monthly payments when the insured reaches a certain age. Used to supplement retirement income.

Estoppel. To stop or "close one's mouth to admit the truth."

Eviction. The legal process used to force one from rented premises.

Evidence.   That which is elicited from the testimony of witnesses in court.

Execution.   A legal process used to collect assets of a judgment debtor and to apply them to the judgment.

Executive sessions.   Closed meetings of members of a board of a corporation

F

Fair trade laws.   Laws designed to permit prices at retail to be established by the manufacturer.

Financing statement.   The "notice document" used under Article 9 of the Uniform Commercial Code.

Fixing damages.   Establishing the actual loss caused by a breach of contract.

Fixtures.   Items of personal property that become part of real estate after installation. For example, a water heater.

Foreclosure.   To execute legal rights after default in a secured transaction.

Forfeiture.   To give up property rights, usually for failure to pay taxes or money.

Franchise.   A contract given by one to another authorizing a certain activity in a certain area.

Fraud.   An intentional misrepresentation of a material fact that misleads another to that person's detriment.

Freedom of contract.   A theoretical privilege that we have to contract as we wish. In practice the right is restricted.

Fungible goods.   Goods that are incapable of being separated once comingled. For example, wheat in a grain elevator.

G

Garnishment.   A legal process whereby the goods or money of one is attached while in the hands of another.

Grantee.   The one to whom a grant, such as a deed, is made.

Grantor. The one who grants something, such as one who deeds property to another.

H

Hearsay evidence. Testimony based upon the statements of one who is not in court.

Holder in due course. In commercial paper, a preferred position that is free of certain defenses.

Holding company. A company that holds stock in another company.

I

Independent contractor. One who agrees to complete work free of control of another.

Injunction. An equitable remedy used to cause one to refrain from a designated activity or action.

Insurable interest. That which one person has in the life of another when that person stands to gain from the continuance, rather than the loss, of that life.

Intestator. One who dies without a will.

Investment securities. Article 8 of the Uniform Commercial Code, stocks and bonds.

J

Joint payees. Two or more people having the same negotiable instrument payable to them.

Joint stock company. An early attempt to limit liability in business by the use of the contract.

Joint venture. An undertaking in which one or more persons combine labor and capital to achieve a single result.

Judgment by default. A court order entered when a defendant fails to set up a defense within the prescribed time period.

K

Kiting.   Raising the amount of a negotiable instrument.

L

Law.   Body of legal and related sanctions that can be enforced in a court.

Common law.   Historically, the law of England. Today, the rulings of courts in the states.

Private law.   Body of legal principles that controls disputes arising between individuals.

Lease.   A contract between a landowner and a lessee, spelling out rights of both.

Legal entity.   Something that has a separate existence in contemplation of law. For example, a corporation.

Legal notice.   An advertisement published in newspapers of general circulation and concerned with legal matters.

Lessee.   The one to whom real estate is leased.

Lessor.   The one who leases real estate to a lessee.

Liability.   As used in law, "responsibility."

Absolute liability.   Responsibility without permitting a defense.

Contract liability.   Responsibility for failure to keep promises.

Joint liability.   Responsibility that rests upon two or more at the same time.

Joint and several liability.   Responsibility that can be laid upon two or more or any one of them.

Limited liability.   Responsibility that is restricted in amount. Found in partnership and corporate law.

Tort liability.   Responsibility for wrongful damages to another's person or property.

Unlimited liability.   In partnership law, responsibility that has no limits.

License.   A right or privilege granted to one by another.

Lien. A claim against real estate, usually arising out of some court action.

Loss leading. Selling items at low prices to attract customers into a store.

M

Maker. Commercial paper. The one who creates a note and signs it.

Merger. For corporations, a joining of firms.

Minor. In contract law, one under the age of majority.

Minority suits. For corporations, litigation instituted by stockholders.

Minutes. For corporations, written records of meetings.

Misrepresentation. An unintentional misleading of one person by another to that person's detriment.

Mistake. In law, a justifiable reason for setting aside a contract.

Mitigation of damages. A legal requirement in contract law that one "keep down" the damages of the one who has breached a contract.

Monopoly. A business situation in which one person or a firm "captures" and controls a market to its advantage.

Mortgage. An encumbrance against real estate that arises out of a secured loan obtained from a lending institution.

Motion. A spoken or printed request under parliamentary procedure addressed to a judge (or presiding officer) seeking a ruling on the point raised.

Mutuality. In contract law, the state of being in agreement upon particulars.

N

Negligence. Failure to exercise due care.

Negotiability. In commercial paper, that quality of transferability unhampered by any restraints.

Negotiable instruments. Those instruments covered by Article 3 of the Uniform Commercial Code.

Net profit. Gains after all costs are taken into consideration.

Note. Commercial paper. A written promise to pay.

Novation. Substitution of debtors, debt, or creditors. For example, A owes B $100, and C agrees to pay B because B owes A $100.

O

Offer. In contract law, a proposal of what one is willing to do in a contract setting.

Offeree. The one to whom a contract offer is made.

Offeror. The one who makes a contract offer.

Option. A contract that binds one to hold an offer open for a specified period of time for an agreed-upon price.

Order paper. Commercial paper. Negotiable instruments that must be endorsed before they can be negotiated.

Order to pay. Commercial paper. One requirement of negotiable paper usually met by the word "pay."

Ordinance. Municipal law. A law created by a city council.

P

Parol. Evidence rule. In contract law, a rule of long standing that prohibits a written contract to be changed by oral testimony.

Partnership. An association of two or more persons to carry on, as coowners, a business for profit.

Implied partnership. A partnership created by the acts of the parties.

Interest in the firm. One of the property rights of a partner.

Limited partnership. A firm in which the liability of one or more partners is restricted to each partner's capital contribution.

Partnership agreement. A contract used to form a partnership.

Partnership property. That which is owned by a partnership, including real and personal property.

Silent partner. A partner with limited liability who cannot take an active part in the operation of a partnership.

Specific partnership property. That which is owned by the partners as partners and thus beyond the reach of individual creditors.

Tenants in partnership. A legal phrase to describe how partners own "specific partnership" property.

Patent. A protective process provided by the government to reserve to one for a stated period the fruits of one's creations.

Payee. Commercial paper. The one to whom negotiable instruments are made payable.

Perfection. Secured transactions. That stage at which one's security interest is completed to the fullest extent provided by law.

Possession. Custody that is either "actual" or "constructive."

Postdating. Commercial paper. Dating a negotiable instrument ahead, usually a check, thus making it a "time instrument."

Power of attorney. A formal "agency" in which the principal grants specified authority to an "agent."

Preemptive right. Corporation law. A right of stockholders to purchase a proportionate share of any new stock issues.

Prepayment without release. A program followed by some insurance companies of making advance payment to the other party injured by their insured.

Price concessions. The granting of price deductions for quantity purchases.

Price fixing. Unlawful price maintenance by firms that would normally be in competition with each other.

Price leading. A system of lawful price maintenance in which competing firms follow price raises by one of the firms.

Prima facie. "On the face of it." In trial work, evidence that is sufficient to establish a case or right of recovery, but which can be rebutted.

Principal. In agency law, the one who grants authority to an agent.

Priority. Secured transactions. What one secured party has that gives it better claim to collateral than another secured party that claims the same collateral.

Privity. In contract law, the relation created when one contracts with another. The term means "closeness" in contract law.

Probate. The system of administering the estate of a deceased person, including payment of debts, taxes, and fees.

Promise to pay. Commercial paper. A phrase required in notes.

Promissory note. Often used to describe a note created under Article 3 of the Uniform Commercial Code.

Promotor. For corporations, one who lays the groundwork and sees that the proper procedures are followed to create a new corporation.

Property. The earth and all property rights that exist with it.

Personal property. Property that is not affixed to the earth. For example, one's watch, shoes, car, and furniture in the home.

Real property. The earth and everything permanently affixed to it.

Proprietorship. An unincorporated business owned and frequently operated by one person.

Proxy. For corporations, written authority granted by one stockholder to another to vote the first stockholder's stock. An agency.

Q

Quitclaim deed. A conveyance of real estate in which the grantor conveys whatever interest the grantor may have, which in fact may be none. Widely used to clear up doubts in real property titles.

R

Ratification. A later adoption of an act that was unauthorized when committed.

Reasonable person. The ordinary person acting in the conduct of personal affairs. A measuring stick used widely in court.

Rebate. A "kickback," or return of part of a purchase price of goods or services.

Release. A contract designed to free one from further legal claims of another.

Remuneration. Wages or payment for services.

Repossession. Secured transactions. The act of retaking secured collateral because of default in payment on a loan.

Rescission. Canceling or taking back.

Retainer. A fee paid in advance for services to be performed.

Revocation. The canceling of an offer after it has been made but before it has been accepted.

Right of way. A legal right granted by an owner to another to cross or use a portion of one's land.

S

Secondary meaning. In trade name law, a word or words that have become identified with a firm or its products so as to become entitled to trade name protection.

Secured transactions. That body of law spelled out in Article 9 of the Uniform Commercial Code as well as secured loans made where real estate is used as security.

Securities.   Stocks and bonds.

Security agreement.   A legal document used under Article 9 of the Uniform Commercial Code to grant a security interest and to spell out terms of the loan.

Security interest.   That which is granted to a lender as security in collateral used in a loan.

Security or collateral.   That which is used as assurance that a loan will be repaid.

Sharking.   An unscrupulous practice of making loans at excessive rates of interest.

Slander.   Spoken defamation.

Small claims court.   Tribunals created to decide small disputes.

Specific performance.   In contract law, a remedy in equity designed to force one to keep contract promises.

Standard of care.   The level of caution that one should exercise.

Statute of frauds.   Acts of legislatures that require certain contractual matters to be in writing and signed by the person to be charged by them.

Statute of limitations.   Acts or legislatures stating time limits within which suits may be brought.

Stock.   For corporations, that which is owned by shareholders and which represents a unit of interest in the firm.

   Bonus stock.   Stock given as an incentive to purchase stock in a firm. Sometimes the phrase refers to an unlawful overissue of stock.

   Capital stock.   The issued stock of a corporation and the value received by the sale of the same.

   Common stock.   Stock held in common with others. The most predominant type of stock.

   Cumulative stock.   Preferred stock for which preference accumulates until it is paid.

   Founder's (promoter's) stock.   Stock used to pay for the services of one who creates a corporation.

Noncumulative stock. Preferred stock that loses its preference in any year the preference is not paid.

Nonparticipating stock. Preferred stock that is entitled to preference but to nothing else.

Nopar stock. Stock that does not have a stated value.

Participating stock. Preferred stock with an additional feature permitting it to share in some ratio with common stock after it receives its preference.

Preferred stock. A type of stock that has an "edge" or preference over common stock.

Share of stock. The intangible portion of ownership of a corporation.

Stock certificate. A piece of paper that is evidence of the underlying shares in a corporation.

Stockholder. One who owns a portion of a corporation.

Stock split. A redesignation of the number of shares and par value of outstanding shares of stock.

Stock subscriptions. A contract to buy stock in a corporation after it is formed.

Stock warrants. A certificate issued by a corporation giving specified rights to the stockholders.

Stop payment. In Article 4 of the Uniform Commercial Code, the process of alerting a drawee bank and requesting that the bank not honor a check already issued.

Subagent. In agency law, an agent hired by one who is an agent of a principal.

Sum certain. Commercial paper. An amount that is precise or can be calculated precisely at any given moment.

Surety. One who agrees to pay an obligation if another does not.

Surety bond. A legal document by which one promises to back a money promise made by another.

Surplus. For corporations, an excess of assets over liabilities plus capital stock.

T

Tenancy.   The legal ownership that one has in the real property of another by virtue of being a tenant.

Tenancy at will.   A tenancy that can be discontinued at any time by the lessor or lessee by giving proper notice.

Tenants in common.   A legal status in which two or more persons own the same real estate at the same time.

Termination.   To end or bring to a conclusion.

Testator.   A person who leaves a will.

Title.   A status that carries with it legal rights and privileges.

   Equitable title.   Title that is grounded in equity.

   Legal title.   Title grounded in law. One who holds a deed to land has the legal title.

Trademark.   A distinctive mark used in business that is entitled to protection.

Trade name.   A distinctive name used in business that is entitled to protection.

Trespass.   The act of going upon or over another's land without permission. Also refers to an attack upon another.

Trust.   An arrangement in which certain powers are granted to a trustee.

Trustee.   One who serves for the benefit of designated beneficiaries in a trust.

Truth in lending.   A requirement of Title 1, C.C.P.A.

U

Undue influence.   An overactive forcing of one's will upon another.

Unemployment compensation.   A form of insurance created to assist those who are without work.

Unenforceable.   Cannot be enforced.

Unfair competition.   In business, conduct that exceeds the normal bounds of competition.

Uniform Commercial Code.   An extensive body of business laws adopted by 49 states.

Uniform laws. Written laws designed to be adopted by every state legislature without modification.

Unjust enrichment. The gaining of wealth in a manner that is oppressive to the one from whom the wealth is taken.

Usury. The charging of more interest than the law allows.

V

Valid. Good. Effective.

Void. Invalid. Worthless.

Voidable. Subject to cancellation. Good but can be avoided.

Voting. For corporations, the act of stating one's position on an issue.

W

Wage attachment. Garnishment. A legal proceeding used to pay a judgment out of one's wages.

Warranty. In contract law, a promise that relates to the quality of goods. Also promises made in the use of commercial paper.

Warranty liability. Responsibiity that arises out of contract or commercial paper promises.

Will. A testamentary document by which one disposes of one's estate upon death.

Winding up. In partnership law, that stage in the life of a firm where all assets are liquidated and all bills paid.

Without recourse. Commercial paper. An endorsement by which an endorser disclaims any warranty liability.

Workers' compensation. A "no fault" procedure designed to compensate one who is injured on the job.

Z

Zoning. A systematic alignment of real property and its uses. Designed to protect property values.

INDEX